C708 019 037 409 CB

903

PLEASE ~~~~~~ THIS BOOK IN ANY
CALVERTON
(Hold)

13. APR 11
15 SEP 2015
27 NOV 2015

WITHDRAWN

ENJOY AN
ROUP

24 Hour Renewal Service
Phone 0845 330 4435

Nottingham Central Library
Floor 3

City Library
Department of Leisure and Community Services

The last date entered is the date by which
the book must be returned. You can renew
books by phoning or visiting the Library.

Nottingham City Council

ANN MOORE

Published in England 2007

by Eyelevel Books, Worcester

www.eyelevelbooks.co.uk

ISBN 9781902528236

Copyright © Ann Moore 2007

Foreword © Bill Maynard 2007

Illustrations © Diane Cope 2007

The right of contributors to be identified as the authors of this work has been asserted by them in accordance with the Copyright, Designs and Patents Act 1998. All rights reserved. No part of this publication may be reproduced, stored or introduced into a retrieval system or transmitted in any form or by any means without the prior written permission of the publisher.

A CIP catalogue record for this book is available from the British Library

Typeset and Designed by Eyelevel Books.

Printed and bound in Great Britain by Biddles Ltd, King's Lynn

CONTENTS

SECTION 1 SETTING THE FOUNDATIONS

1   How to Begin   3
Objectives; Membership; Group meetings; Company Name

2   Setting a Foundation   13
The Committee; The Constitution; Funding; Fund-raising

3   Drama Activities   19
Group meetings; Format for Meetings; Other activities;

4   Rules and Regulations   27
Copyright; Royalties; Photocopying; Video recording

5   Thinking Ahead   29
Staging a Production; The Business Side of a Production; Publicity and Marketing; Front of House

SECTION 2 SHOWTIME

6   Planning a Production   53
Choice of Production; Considering a Play

7   Theatre-Speak   61
Technical terms

8   Setting The Scene   65
Production Profiles; The Production Team; Producer/Director; Set designer; Wardrobe Mistress; Lighting technician; Sound technician; Property Master; Other Specialists

9   Stage Management   87
The Stage Management Team; Assistant and Deputy Stage Managers

10   From Page to Stage   94
The Role of the Director; Casting the Play; Blocking; Rehearsals; Director's Checklist; First Night and Beyond

11   Notes for the Actor   125
Questions often Asked; Establishing Character; Learning Lines

SECTION 3 ACQUIRING SKILLS AND CONFIDENCE

12	Introduction	141
	Acquiring Skills; Tips for the Leader	
13	Warm-ups	144
	Ice-breakers; Circle games; Space Activities; Imagination	
14	Concentrate!	154
	The Need for Concentration; Activities to Aid Concentration	
15	Relax…	159
	The Need for Relaxation; Activities to Aid Relaxation	
16	Performance Skills 1	164
	Vocal Performance Skills; Breath Control; Articulation; Vocal Expression; Projection	
17	Performance Skills 2	175
	Physical Performance Skills; Body Language; Creating Character Physically; Memory and Imagination	
18	Creative Drama	183
	Improvisation and Mime;	
17	Improvised Drama	192
	Appendix – useful web sites	209
	Index	211

ACKNOWLEDGMENTS

I should like to express my thanks to the following: Jon at Eyelevel Books for suggesting that I write the book in the first place and for his subsequent encouragement and patience; to Diane Cope for her delightful drawings; to John Hackett for his suggestions and for proof-reading; to Shiela Hodges and Jake Chambers for checking some of the information. For their valued support in this project I must also thank the veteran professional actor Bill Maynard and the Chairman of the Independent Theatre Council, Gavin Stride, who are both great advocates of amateur participation in the arts. I must also mention the actors and directors, both amateur and professional with whom, over the years, I have enjoyed the happiest of times and from whom I learned so much. Finally my thanks must go to my family who allowed me time and space, not only to pursue my interests in drama, but also to produce this book.

ABOUT THE AUTHOR

Ann Moore has been involved with drama for more than fifty years, experiencing most aspects of the art, from acting to stage management, props to directing.

Working with both amateurs and professionals, she has acted in more than fifty plays, from Alan Ayckbourn and Agatha Christie to Shakespeare and Arnold Wesker.

She has directed regularly for the last thirty years – and still does – and has taught drama to Secondary School pupils and adults.

She is an active member of two Performing Arts groups, one of which is based in a professional theatre, and she recently established a thriving drama society in her local community.

FOREWORD BY BILL MAYNARD

Having spent a lifetime as a professional in most aspects of the entertainment business, I read this guide to amateur drama by Ann Moore with great interest.

This straightforward, all-embracing manual is perfect for anyone who is interested in the stage as a hobby but has little experience. Yet there are ideas here which would interest the more experienced members of an amateur drama group too – and the tips are not just for actors. The spotlight of information is turned on all aspects of amateur drama, from starting up a group in the first place to staging a production and covering everything from improvising acting skills to the work of the director and stage management and to those involved with their audience front-of-house.

Whatever your interest in amateur drama you'll find ideas in this manual which will help you to enjoy not only the fun and friendship, but also the *success*, as you share your love of the stage to bring live theatre into your community.

Bill Maynard, 2007

AUTHOR'S NOTE

Every actor and every director has his own way of working and in writing this book I pass on ideas which have worked for me and for many others, both amateur and professional with whom I have been associated in drama. Take from them what you will.

In an attempt to avoid over-long and cumbersome descriptions, I have compromised in my use of pronouns. I have often referred, for example, to the Director as 'he'; to the Stage Manager as 'she'; and so on. This should not be taken as bias and readers should never infer that these, or any other, roles are better suited to one or the other. All jobs, from committee chair and director right through to coffee-server and programme seller are, and should be, considered as equally suitable for *anyone* with the skill and willingness to undertake them.

Amateur Drama is one of the most democratic and inclusive art-forms and it is a place to leave politics and prejudice at the door. Disability, colour, educational background or sex are no barrier to participation within any of the huge range of jobs necessary to bring drama to the stage. For both participants and audience it should be the fun and life-enhancing experience which I have always found it to be. The stage is a world of dreams where anything is possible, whoever you are.

So, Beginners, Please, take your place, have fun and let the dream begin…

SECTION 1

SETTING THE FOUNDATIONS

1 HOW TO BEGIN

what this chapter covers...

Amateur drama can flourish in a wide variety of settings. In this chapter we look at how to set your group on its first steps towards becoming a long-term, thriving drama company, whatever your setting and whoever your prospective members may be.

We look briefly at the where and when of group meetings and consider the importance of the group's name.

INTRODUCTION

Being a member of an amateur drama group can be fun and very rewarding, but there may not be one in your area and setting up a group from scratch, finding out just how to begin, can be a daunting prospect. This book aims to pass on basic, practical advice, born of experience, to anyone who, with like-minded people in their community, wishes to form such a group. It may be in an urban area or a village; it may be for children or for youth, for adults who are still working or for those who are retired. For those using amateur drama within an organisation – school or prison for example – some of the information may not be needed, although Sections 2 and 3, concerning performance organisation and drama technique, are applicable to drama in any setting. Whenever amateur drama is practised, both participants and audience benefit from the social interaction and the enjoyment which the Arts can give. Members of the group will learn new skills, make new friends and gain in a confidence which should carry through into other aspects of their lives. But how do you begin?

A STARTING POINT

The process generally begins in a small way by the coming together of a few people, wherever they live, who are interested in forming an amateur drama group. They may have had a little experience or none at all, but they all have a wish to meet socially and see if, together, they could put on some entertainment which everyone in their community would enjoy. Hopefully, at least one member of this interested party will be someone with management skills and some knowledge of drama, someone who would be prepared to act as organiser of the meetings and possibly of any production which may later be decided upon.

Discussion as to the viability of the project can begin over coffee and biscuits in someone's living room, where ideas can be discussed and decisions made in a friendly, social atmosphere – unless, of course, there is sufficient interest within the community to merit the cost of hiring a hall at this early stage, in which case you may wish to advertise locally for even more members.

Subsequent meetings – for business matters, play readings or individual rehearsals for one or two actors perhaps – may be held in members' homes, especially in the beginning, but as the group grows in membership and ambition, space will be needed to allow movement. Rehearsing round someone's lounge furniture is not really a sensible option unless the play has a cast of only two or three people.

For the purpose of this exercise, we shall call this small group of like-minded people the steering group who, although not at this stage constituting the formal committee, (which will be a necessary part of the group, see p14), will make the decisions needed to get the project off the ground. The leader, or organiser, will be referred to as 'he', an old convention but one which is in no way meant to imply that a woman could not do the job just as well. Indeed, there are many women who, having both management skills and a knowledge of the theatre, prove to be great organisers and leaders in the field of drama, both amateur and professional.

OBJECTIVES

The steering group should first decide on what kind of dramatic art they wish to promote – plays or musical theatre. For the latter they will need someone who has the ability to produce this specialised art form, which incorporates, as well as acting, music and dance. For the purposes of this book, we shall assume that the performance of plays within the local community will be the new group's main objective.

Below are the aims which any amateur drama group will hope to achieve, whether the group is small, working in a village hall, or larger, perhaps as the resident amateur company working within a professional theatre. The steering group should have in mind that they wish:

1. To form a social, non-profit making group concentrating on the art and enjoyment of drama, which, meeting regularly in a venue to be decided, will benefit the local community. (Non-profit making does not mean that the group will find itself in debt, merely that it will not accrue a vast bank account. Instead, it will aim to sustain a cash-flow which will be sufficient to keep it viable, while at the same time being in a position to make some donation towards a charitable cause, if so desired by the membership.)

2. To promote and encourage the appreciation of all aspects of theatre through an active participation in drama, play readings, talks and visits to theatres and other drama groups.

3. To enhance this appreciation by learning acting technique through creative activities, workshops and productions.

4. To encourage the knowledge and use of the practical and organisational skills, other than acting, which are used in drama – ie. stage design and workshop, costume and its history, properties and set dressing, the effective use of lighting and sound, publicity and front of house work – in effect all the backstage and other skills needed to stage a production.

5. To maintain an open-door policy towards membership and, through this and performance, to link with the general community.

6. To present public performances of drama to the highest possible standard, so that the group, and its work, is shown in a favourable light.

7. To ensure that the meetings and all work undertaken by the group is carried out in a sociable and friendly environment, which encourages members to try something new when they feel ready to do so, so helping them grow in confidence and ability and enabling them to work together as a team to realise any set goal.

MEMBERSHIP

In any community there are two different age groups for whom a drama group might be formed: adults and children (under 16).

Adults

Most groups are made up of people who join initially because they have an interest in drama. They may be men or women, young or of middle age, employed or unemployed, older or retired. All female groups can, and do, flourish, whether they are part of a larger organisation – as in Women's Institutes – or not, although the choice of play is more limited where there are no male actors. In every case, however, joining any socially based group, and drama is no exception, can make people feel part of the community in which they live and can lead to new friendships.

The steering group should endeavour to ensure that:

1. Membership is open to anyone of adult age, male and female, able and disabled, regardless of race and religion, and that all members understand that an amateur drama group is a non-political organisation.

2. Anyone who does not wish to act, but who expresses an interest in membership will be welcomed for, as shown in the objectives (no. 4 on p5) many other equally important skills are needed besides the ability to act, particularly when staging a show.

    Fortunate is the group, which can count among its membership those who are happy to come along just to be part of the company, to watch what goes on, make the 'half-time' tea and join in the gossip. Very often unexpected talent can be found, and with encouragement many members find that they can do a lot more than they would ever have believed possible.

3. Members pay the annual fee, which will be set by committee (at first, perhaps by the steering group until a formal committee is chosen) and ratified by the membership.

    The fee should be set at a rate which is not too high to deter membership but high enough to make the group viable, when the cost of hiring the regular meeting venue and other overheads is taken into account. This fee and the membership card (which can be easily designed and printed on a home computer) should be recognised as having value, since it confers membership and acts as a holding stake in the company. Any members failing to pay within a given number of weeks after the annual renewal date (generally 1st April, near the start of the financial year) should be deemed to have terminated their membership.

4. Anyone taking part in a group production must be, for the purposes of insurance, a fully paid-up member.

5. Membership fees and any other company money will be held, on the members' behalf, in a bank account under the group's name, thereby giving the group a legal financial base.

6. If the group wishes to formulate different levels of membership – full, student, patron or friend, for example – it should be understood that too many levels can sometimes be difficult to define accurately and can complicate the work of the treasurer. Rules governing membership in whichever category should be discussed before ratification by the membership and noted in the group's governing document, which will be created as part of its constitution (see p15).

7. Members may attend and take part in decision making at ordinary meetings whenever they are held, especially at the Annual General Meeting when future planning and voting for committee takes place.

8. Any member bringing the group into disrepute (by appearing drunk on stage, for example) or who jeopardises a group undertaking, will be answerable to the committee acting on behalf of the membership, and can expect their membership to be terminated or some other disciplinary action.

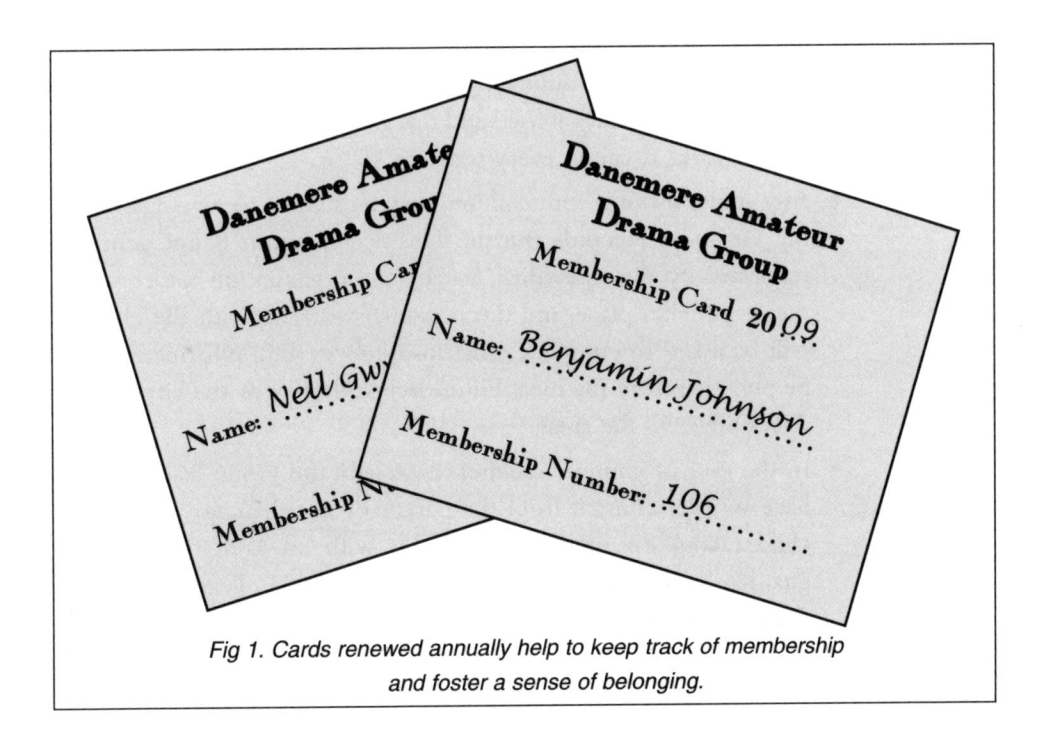

Fig 1. Cards renewed annually help to keep track of membership and foster a sense of belonging.

CHILDREN

This group could be sub-divided for the purposes of an out of school drama group into children of Primary school age – ie aged 5 to 8 and 9 to 11 or 12 – and those aged 12 to 16 who attend Secondary school. Many parents whose children express a wish to learn drama pay fees to register them in to a local drama school, many working in the age ranges above, or on to a course run by a theatre. Others are able to take part in plays at a Youth Centre. So as a general rule, drama for children is organised and run by drama specialists or those who have worked with children in a teaching situation, and the rules governing this are stringent. Therefore,

1. Any amateur drama group asked to have children as part of its membership, or wishing to set up a group specifically for children of whatever age, would be well advised to contact first the local authority's Education Welfare or Children's Services department for guidance, and to have as their leader a member who has a good knowledge of drama with, preferably, teaching skills. They should be able to encourage an interest in the Arts and engage with children or young people in a happy, yet disciplined atmosphere. It can be demanding work, but very rewarding.

2. Anyone considering such a move should also know that Government Child Protection policies demand that a child's safety, both physical and emotional, must be paramount at all times. The group leader has a duty of care to ensure that children are not verbally or physically abused and that the environment in which the group works is safe in every respect.

3. Any adult working with children may be subject to investigation by the Criminal Records Bureau. This accreditation is not generally requested by the individual, but by the organisation under which the work takes place, and the person(s) working with the children will be asked to complete a disclosure form. Full information may be obtained from the local Education Authority or the city/county Arts Officer in the area.

4. In the case of younger children especially, the group leader should have written consent from the parent or guardian agreeing to the child taking on membership, along with an assurance that the guardian will be responsible for delivering and collecting the child from the meetings at times to be specified. This consent form should also note any disability or health problem which the child may have,

with specific agreement for any emergency treatment which may be necessary while the child is in the care of the group. This form, which should include the guardian's address with the home telephone number, (and an emergency number if it is different) should be kept in a safe, easily accessible place within the group.

5. In the event of a public performance, the group leader must ensure that children are under the supervision of a responsible adult acting as chaperone, especially when not on stage.

6. Unless it is part of a school event, children under 16 may not take part in any public performance for more than four nights unless a licence has been obtained from the local authority, and application for this should be made a month before rehearsals begin. Again, full information should be obtained from one of the authorities above or the local council's Education Welfare service.

7. Neither rehearsals nor performance should continue to a late hour and it must be understood that being a member of any drama group should not affect a child's welfare or impinge on school work.

GROUP MEETINGS – VENUE

Drama can take place anywhere there is a space, whether it is in a hall, a church or a school, in the street or in a garden, but regular group meetings need a suitable indoor venue. They cannot always be held in someone's home, so the group will need to find a venue large enough in which to meet regularly and eventually to rehearse. This does not generally present a problem in the case of a school-based group or where members of a prison population is involved, but finding space in a suitable community hall in an urban or village area can be more difficult. The hall will be there, but doubtless it will be well used and so booking a space on a regular basis may not be easy. It is essential that dates, whether for ordinary meetings or for performance, are always booked well in advance. School halls are sometimes available for use by members of the public, but in some areas rental charges are high. Enquiries must be made of the local town or parish council, village hall committee or the relevant education authority as to cost and availability of any space.

At this stage, the steering committee will be looking for a venue for regular meetings, but requirements for performance space are included here as well, in the hope that any available venue will also be suitable for staging shows. If this is the case, the group is indeed fortunate, for members will be familiar with its layout and the committee will know just how suitable it would be for the performance it plans to stage.

Several points should be borne in mind before making a decision on a venue. It is not intended that this list should stop anyone holding those first vital meetings at home – meetings which will launch them into the fun that is amateur drama – but questions to bear in mind are:

1. Is the floor area large enough for members to move around easily when engaging in practical work or working in separate small groups? Are available chairs and tables stackable and easily moved?
2. Is there a stage? It goes without saying that for any drama group this is a valuable amenity, although it's not vital for regular meetings.
3. Where is the venue in relation to the potential membership?

    Does it have its own car park, is there one nearby, or is it on a bus route?

    Is it in a safe, well-lit area? – members wouldn't enjoy walking down a dark alley at any time of the year.

    Is the venue itself in an orderly and safe state of repair?
4. Facilities – obviously there will be a toilet block, but is there a kitchen? This is to be a social drama group, after all, so a break for tea or coffee will be part of the package.
5. Are the entrances and toilets suitable for the disabled? These considerations are particularly important if this meeting place is to welcome all potential members and/or is where you hope to stage shows for the public.
6. Does rental include the cost of heating and lighting?
7. Would you be meeting in a room next to another where a choir or band practice, for example, might be taking place at the same time as your meeting? Conversely, would your activities disturb a study group next door?
8. Who would be responsible for locking and unlocking the hall? If you should have exclusive use of the venue, which is unlikely, it would be wise to have some form of written contract so that the group knows exactly what its responsibilities are. You may wish to have this form of security whatever your rental situation may be.
9. The licensee will have rules of usage – whether the venue is licensed for public performance, for example – and matters relevant to insurance and health and safety, and you should enquire exactly what these are.

[10] It is here worth noting that eventually, when the group is organised and active, it should carry insurance against personal accident and loss or damage to person or property during meetings. You should also make sure that you (or the owner of the property) are covered for public liability when staging a public performance. Full information can be obtained from an insurance company, preferably one which deals with theatre, or from the relevant web site on p209.

[11] Although storage may not be a factor at this early stage, bear in mind that as the group consolidates, amateur drama can present problems of this nature. Many groups, such as those meeting for talks or card games, only need tables and chairs, which most venues have anyway, but once a drama group starts working on productions it gathers about it 'extras' which need to be stored. These may include costume, properties and even odd pieces of furniture which other people willingly give 'if you have somewhere to keep it', to say nothing of the possibility of scenery, flats or curtains. So, after a while, members' attics and garages begin to overflow and storage space becomes a necessity. Finding somewhere dry, not too far away, not too expensive and preferably with electric light, may become a problem. Better to have this in mind from the beginning, although such a consideration should never prevent the formation of a new group.

GROUP MEETINGS – WHEN?

The availability and cost of renting space for meetings may be a factor in determining how often and for how long the group will meet, especially at first. Most groups meet weekly or fortnightly. If meeting in the evening the preferred time is usually from 7.30 until 9.30 or 10pm. To meet only once a month has been found not to be sufficiently often to sustain interest for people with busy lives. Meeting regularly on the same evening at the same time becomes a habit, ensures that enthusiasm is less likely to fade and members will look forward to meeting their new friends socially as well as coming together to learn drama skills or work towards a production. When building up to a production, of course, rehearsals will need to be held more frequently, and often those which do not involve all the cast can be held in someone's lounge or dining room – or even the garden, if space and weather allow.

NAME

The name under which the group shall meet and work should be decided as early as possible, but not necessarily by the steering group. It could – and often does – arise out of discussion by the general membership during the first few meetings, and it is better if it is a joint decision and not one imposed by the organiser(s). That name, however, should be original, reflect the aims and status of the group and should not be one which is the same, or might be confused with, that of another drama company, amateur or professional.

2 SETTING A FOUNDATION

what this chapter covers...

Even very early in the process of setting up a drama group, it is worth considering organisational aspects such as *committees*, a working *constitution* and issues of *funding*. If you are aware of these from the outset – and deal with them in a timely fashion – you will be freer to run and enjoy the group in the long term.

SETTING A FOUNDATION FOR THE FUTURE

The initial meetings will have seen members of the steering group do a great deal of work toward organising its new drama company. Even if originally they only came together with the specific idea of performing a certain play, there must come a time, whatever the group's original concept, when they must set the group on a firm and permanent foundation.

This requires the setting up of a business committee and the formulation of a governing document, which will become the group's Constitution. There are those who advise organisers to have a formal Constitution from the beginning, but too many hard and fast rules in the earliest stages have been known to stifle enthusiasm. Better, perhaps, to wait until several meetings have been enjoyed, founding members have come to know each other, have decided on their achievable objects and know that they wish to continue as a group. Then, committee members could be proposed and voted in by the membership and, after discussion, they will formulate the constitution to be agreed and voted upon by all members at a general meeting. So, the company will have set itself on a firm foundation with members knowing that they belong to a well-organised group, which can move forward into the future with confidence.

THE COMMITTEE

In addition to the leader (or president/director as he might become), the group will require a committee to undertake day-to-day administrative tasks. This will leave the leader time to concentrate on organising and running the regular meetings and any productions which will be undertaken. Committee meetings need not be held on a strictly regular basis, but can be called as and when necessary with a minimum of two each year. However, this committee must summon an Annual General Meeting – generally at the beginning of the group's financial year – which all members are invited to attend. The committee may also, on occasion, need to call all members to a meeting if decisions need to be made which involve the group.

Most committees consist of group members, proposed, seconded and voted into the posts for a given length of time by the membership. The committee members could be changed or stand again each year, but there should be a finite time during which they may serve. It is advisable, in the case of officers particularly, that they do not all stand for re-election at the same time. Rather, if their re-election is staggered there will be a continuity of management within the company.

The committee should consist of the following two sub-groups.

OFFICERS

The officers of a committee hold the honorary posts of:

Chairman, who chairs both committee meetings and ordinary business meetings attended by the general membership, and is generally the spokesman for the group.

Secretary, who gives notice of, and takes Minutes at all business meetings, handles correspondence and keeps a record of the group's activities.

Treasurer, who holds all moneys, including the membership fees, keeps accounts of all income and expenditure, has the power, with one other signatory, to write and receive cheques on behalf of the group and prepares an annual statement of account, which should be audited each year.

ORDINARY MEMBERS

Ordinary members chosen to represent the group on the committee may consist of whatever number is thought to be necessary, and this is generally between three and six in number – large committees can be unwieldy – but during its term of office the committee should have the power to co-opt members to provide an extra skill, or to fill a vacancy if a committee member has had to leave. The co-opted member would serve until the next Annual General Meeting when, with the agreement of the general membership, he may then become a full committee member if there is a vacancy, or stand against others if there is an election.

As well as representing their fellow members, ordinary committee members may also take on the roles of leaders of any sub-committees which may be appointed to fulfil any special needs at the time – as for, example, when a production is envisaged. They may then be responsible for organising publicity, ticket selling, interval catering and front of house duties etc for the duration of the project.

It is the committee which makes decisions on behalf of the general membership on any business which affects the group, before seeking permission from the membership for any action it may wish to take on their behalf.

It is also the committee, with the leader and members of the steering group (if they are not part of the committee) who formulate the rules and regulations, which will become the group's governing document, otherwise known as the Constitution. This they must set before the general membership for ratification.

THE CONSTITUTION

This document is a written record governing how the group is and should be run. It should

- Set out the group's name, its definition as an amateur drama group and the age range for which it is formed (adult or children), the community in which it is organised and its meeting place at the time of ratification.
- State the group's aims and objectives.
- Explain the make-up of the committee as the management group, how and when it is elected, the period of time each committee member may serve and how many members present represents a quorum for the purpose of decision making, the work which the committee should undertake on behalf of the membership and the powers which it holds.

- List the rules for general membership of the group, none of whom should receive any remuneration unless for professionally related work. (This is particularly important should the group later wish to apply for charitable status). The rules should state the lowest age at which membership may begin and if there are any categories other than full, active membership, noting the annual subscription for each of these categories, if applicable, along with the annual date when subscriptions should be paid, and reasons for the possible dismissal of a group member. The procedures to be followed for dismissal should be set down in case such action is found to be necessary.
- Set down rules for the holding of meetings for the general membership, they having been given at least three weeks notice of said meeting. Decisions may only be taken at these general meetings if there is at least a quorum present – generally 40% of the membership.
- Note any limitation of liability by the group in the case of damage, injury or theft involving members or the general public.
- Set down rules for the closure of the group if, for some reason, dissolution becomes unavoidable, along with detail of what should become of any assets, including money, which the group holds at the time of dissolution.

If it is necessary for the constitution to be altered or added to in any way, the membership must be called to an Extraordinary General Meeting, at which they will be asked to ratify any proposed change.

Taking the time to set the company on a firm and legal footing should bring many advantages. Not only will members feel confidence because they are part of an organised company, but the community, too, will share that confidence and be ready to support whatever the group does in the future.

FUNDING

Those with money at their disposal for the furtherance of the Arts, especially Arts in the Community, will look much more favourably on an amateur group which

- Is well organised, having documents which govern its position and status, a committee, and audited, annual accounts of its financial affairs.

- Is set up with social, possibly educational, aims which will benefit the community through the Arts.
- Gives no remuneration to members (unless for professionally related work stated in the constitution).
- Does not trade – by starting to hire out, for money, its costume or properties, for example.

Even a new group may be able to apply for funding in the form of a grant from the National or its own area Arts Council or from other recognised financial sources. This may be needed to go towards a special event, for professional help of some kind, or for essential equipment. The national Awards for All scheme is often recommended to those thinking of applying for a grant, but these awards demand some percentage of matching funds and for a very new group this may not be feasible, so in the early days, if extra funding is necessary, explore first more local funding bodies. The regional Arts Officer will be able to advise.

The above list also includes some of the criteria for groups which, once consolidated, may wish to apply for charitable status, but if this is the case, it is strongly advised that correct and up to date information and guidance is first obtained from Revenue and Customs or Charity Commissioners.

FUND-RAISING

In addition to holding regular meetings, a new group will undoubtedly have to give thought to the necessary task of fund-raising as a way of securing enough money to start work on their first (and subsequent) productions, for it is highly unlikely that the membership fees alone would sustain this.

This fund raising could take the form of a Jumble, Table-top or Bring and Buy Sale, coffee mornings, a Fayre or other such event, or a small 'launch party' when members could show off some of their skills to a potential audience, while combining this entertainment with some other form of fund raising noted above. Indeed, an event such as this can be most successful, for those attending can see the new group in action, meet some of the members and so will be ready to support a full scale production when it comes along.

Raffles are another way of topping up the funds, especially if members or friends have donated the prizes. These do not have to be too elaborate nor does the organisation of the raffle itself. A book of cloakroom tickets will suffice. The law states that tickets may only be sold during the event, with the prizes (not money) being drawn during the interval or at the end of the show. (See also p49.)

A big lottery organised specifically in aid of the group will need officially printed tickets, which will be sold in the community at times and places other than during a show. Such a lottery must first be registered with the Gaming Board for Great Britain. You may offer larger, more prestigious prizes – and since no more than 50% of the total proceeds may be spent on prizes, it is useful if these are perhaps donated by a local business. Tickets must be printed according to Lottery regulations, they must not cost less than £1, and they must not be sold to anyone under sixteen. For current advice see website address on p209.

This is a very successful way of raising funds, but it requires more organisation than the humble raffle and the licensing authority will need to see a record of the money accrued and spent. So, for a new group, which has not yet produced many shows, it may require more time and effort than the members have to give until they are more established.

Sponsorship

When a show has been decided upon, you could consider asking a local business for help in the form of sponsorship, either in cash or in kind (by supplying you with something which you may need for the show, for example). It is always more effective if any sponsorship can link directly into the theme of your show. But do remember, whenever you receive help from someone outside the group, you should give something in return. It could simply be an acknowledgement for help given, a free advertisement in your programme or tickets for your show. If the group is to flourish, good personal relationships with others in your community are essential right from the beginning

3 DRAMA ACTIVITIES

what this chapter covers...

With the committee in place, the constitution agreed and some funds behind you, it is time to start the fun of running a real, functioning group.

In this chapter we look at the role of the *group leader* and suggest a possible *format for the regular group meetings*. *Other activities* which will be of interest and value to the group are also considered.

DRAMA GROUP MEETINGS

THE ROLE OF THE LEADER

To begin with, there will be one member of the steering group, preferably someone with experience in drama, who will be willing to take over the role of leader once the group has been formed, although as time goes on, others may be willing to organise some of the group evenings or other events, such as fund raising, which may be planned at a later date This help should be welcomed, for if meetings are held weekly and only one person is 'in charge' the load can become heavy, and anyway, a different leader will bring new ideas and further the experience of the group.

For the new leader, or anyone unused to organising an evening of activities for a social drama group, the following tips may prove useful.

- **Structure the evening**. In other words, plan what you intend to do, but be prepared to be flexible, and always have more ideas or material than you think you need.
- **Maintain control** in a friendly, not dictatorial manner. To avoid possible argument or dissent always ensure that each member is clear as to what he is to do.
- **Be sensitive** to the mood of the group and don't plough on with something if, after a while, it is clear that members are not receptive to it.

- **Keep a record** of what you have done and note the activities which appear to be most successful

As well as being organised yourself, you must make it clear from the start that one of the requirements in acting is a willingness to *listen*, and that is a courtesy which members must be prepared to extend to you or to anyone else who wants to speak or who requests silence. Enthusiasm for what they are doing, especially when they are engaged in vocal or physical work carried out in small groups, may make members noisy, and they become so engrossed in the activity that they forget to listen for the next instruction. If this happens, insist on their attention, wait until everyone is quiet before starting to speak, and try to remember that if members were not so obviously enjoying what they were doing, the room would be filled with silence.

If excessive noise becomes a problem, or if during conversation or instruction others raise their voices, resist the temptation to make yourself heard by raising your voice too. If you do that, so will everyone else and soon chaos will ensue. Instead, wait quietly and lower the volume of your voice when you begin to speak. Someone will be eager to hear you and quiet the others, and then you can point out the courtesy that you have already asked for! It is not an easy thing to do, but it does work.

How regular meetings are organised is, of course, down to each leader. Some begin an amateur drama group knowing exactly what they are going to do, whether it is a series of play readings or even, perhaps, a play which they know they can cast with the membership already available. However, regular meetings are best if, as far as is possible, they involve all the members. If he is to run a meeting successfully every week, for months or years, the leader must plan ahead, try to keep the programme varied and know roughly what he wishes to achieve. Experience shows that having a basic format can make the work easier.

For a new group which is not sure how to begin, or for another whose members would like to do something different, the following is an outline of how an evening meeting might progress. The ideas are merely suggestions but they follow a format that has been tried, tested and found to be successful, and it creates the framework for the discipline that is essential for success in theatre. It is assumed that such a set format would be used once the group had settled into its regular meeting space. Many more ideas for group activity and skill learning may be found in Section 3 (p141 onwards).

ONE POSSIBLE FORMAT FOR THE WEEKLY MEETING

We shall assume that the meeting starts at 7.30pm. The leader should endeavour to be there at least ten minutes before that, especially if he is the key holder. From the outset it is best to begin the meetings as near to the designated time as possible. This way members endeavour to be punctual and time is not wasted with the leader having to repeat any business. Throughout the session the leader must be aware of the clock, so that activities can be timed to allow whatever else he has in mind to do, for example to allow members to show and share what they are doing, or to start a new exercise.

1. As members arrive, it is helpful if they each take a chair and sit in a semicircle facing the leader, who can then see each one as he addresses them, and better control any discussion which may arise.

2. The leader begins by briefly announcing any business, notices, dates, etc, giving a little time, if necessary, to any debate and perhaps outlining the evening ahead.

3. Then, since members have had the opportunity of sitting back after their arrival, they should be asked to put their chairs to one side and stand in a space on the floor for a 'warm-up' exercise. The term covers a variety of activities from literally 'warming up' the company through movement or verbal exercises, to games which foster concentration and imagination, and relaxation technique. The main reason for using a 'warm-up', especially when the group has only just been formed, is because it has proved to be a very effective way of breaking down barriers between people who may not know each other very well. At first there may be opposition to the idea and groaning at the thought of having to get up and move, but persevere – after all, it's only for five or ten minutes.

The leader should encourage of course, but also be prepared to allow those who really look nervous to sit it out. Make sure that members know that they can stop if they're not physically able to do what is asked of them or are clearly unhappy. Just watching can make members feel part of the group and in time, if they can, they'll begin to join in. Many of the suggestions found at the beginning of Section 3 will break the ice, relaxing members so that, generally amid laughter, they find they're making new friends, enjoying themselves and finding the confidence which they'll need to work together and later, to act on a stage.

4 Chosen activity. This may be an activity which stands on its own as a training exercise in some acting technique, or it may be the setting up of work which will continue after a coffee break. There are so many drama skills which can be learned under the guise of a game or exercise, and the leader will prepare his activities to fit whichever area of drama he wishes to teach or improve.

It could be something as simple as voice training, the physical awareness of space, the vocal and physical expression of different emotions, or setting an improvisation, giving a short scripted excerpt to practise, or creating a character which will be used later. Any of these activities may be done individually, in pairs or in small groups. (See Section 3 for ideas). While members work, the leader is able to move round, helping and encouraging if necessary, while assessing the time which will be needed to complete the activity.

5 Tea Break or extra 'social time'! The fifteen-minute coffee or tea break generally comes at some time between 8.30 and 9pm, when members can chat over a drink and relax.

6 Continue the activity or begin another. After the break, if it is the continuation of a task, members will 'rehearse' what they have done, before taking it in turns to show it to the others, who will hopefully be generous and encouraging in their applause – *if there are any criticisms they must be constructive*. If the group is large not everyone will have time, or be ready to show what they have done and if this is the case, members should not be allowed to feel they have failed in any way. It is for the leader to decide, in the light of what he hopes to do the following week, whether this work should be carried over, or accepted as having been useful and left unfinished, as exercises sometimes are. The new activity begun after the break could be one done by the group as a whole and completed before the evening ends, or carried over to the next meeting. But whatever the activities are, every member should enjoy what he is doing.

7 Ideally the evening should end with a group activity – like Story Building where in turn members add three lines to build up a group story, or Snap Talks (speaking on a random topic for one minute). However, often enthusiasm for work-in-hand carries on until time runs out and it is a rush to tidy up before the session ends.

Just as it is important to start each meeting on time, the evening should end punctually too. This is important for those with outside commitments or who rely on lifts or busses to get home.

All the activities in Section 3 can be used in many ways, as starter ideas, as exercises, and as skill teaching. They can be mixed and blended together to provide a format which each leader can create for himself, while at the same time adding ideas of his own. So, as the weeks progress, the leader can help members perfect the drama skills that they will need to produce amateur drama to its highest standard. This work can, to some extent, be continued even when rehearsals have begun for a show. There may well be occasions when a certain skill needs to be pointed out, or practised to improve an actor's work. The opening group warm-up could continue, even if it is only to practise relaxation so that everyone begins the evening in a shared activity, before separating to whatever each may be doing as his work towards the production. Without this those not directly involved in acting may become disenchanted, especially if regular meetings are the only time when rehearsals can be held. Better then, that sewing, painting, organising ticket selling or some other activity can be going on quietly in another room or at the back of the hall at the same time, and even if non-actors only stay until coffee time, they will still feel part of what is happening.

OTHER ACTIVITIES

As a social group, members should have the opportunity of engaging in activities linked to drama other than those which are production or workshop based, such as:

THEATRE VISITS

Going out to the theatre, or to see other amateur or professional companies in the area. These social outings can be fun and they have the advantage of allowing members to see what others are doing locally. They will promote discussion as well as, perhaps, bringing new ideas to any drama work which the group undertakes.

TALKS

It is interesting to have visiting speakers come into a group occasionally, whether to talk about their particular skills or to regale the members with tales from the world of drama. The local theatre may have a speaker – the manager or someone who works in the professional company, like the stage manager or wardrobe mistress – who would have time to share some of the tricks of their trade. Then there is local radio, which may have, or know of speakers whose activities are linked to some field of drama, or someone who works in television, or is a master in the art of make-up. If you run out of ideas, other social groups, like the Women's Institute, hold lists of speakers and one of their members may be able to recommend someone suitable. If it is appropriate, opening these talks to the public for a small charge would also benefit the community, as well as adding to the funds you might need to book the speaker in the first place.

WRITING

Writing and performing a **monologue** is an exercise which can be done in one evening and it generally proves to be very interesting. It is most effective if members have first had the opportunity of reading some examples, so that they know how it should be done. Then the request to 'write one yourself' should be made without too much time being given for thought. It need not be too long, and its author may write as himself, or as someone else. (If this exercise is undertaken during rehearsals for a play, it can be very worthwhile to write the monologue 'in character'.) Each author then reads his work aloud to the group. Sometimes the results can be quite enlightening!

Trying to write a **short sketch** can be fun (and it's sometimes a necessity when trying to fill a gap in a variety show!) so once in a while, members may be challenged to write something. This can be done individually or as a group of two or three who could 'brainstorm' ideas first. Sketches may also grow out of improvisation (see p192) and may even become a one-act play.

Finding answers to the questions *Who? What? When? Why?* and *Suppose…* may help here too, or could even be a starting point. But writers should remember that a good plot, like any story, should have a beginning, a middle and a satisfying end – perhaps with a twist, always popular with audiences. Having found interesting characters and the plot, the next step is to write down the framework of the play, while continuing to shape it through repeated improvisation, until at last a script emerges. The dialogue could then be written down, if necessary, while continuing to strengthen and perfect the characters, their relationships and their story.

All this will, of course, take a long time to bring the play up to performance standard, and should therefore begin as an 'in-house' exercise for the mutual enjoyment of members. But it is a very satisfying exercise and a great deal of imagination, acting talent and hidden writing skills may well emerge from within the group.

Play Reading

Play reading is not only the obvious activity for a drama group, it is also popular and very useful. It can serve two functions: it widens the group's knowledge of drama, of the different types of play, and in particular of plays which they may one day stage – and of those they will never be able to stage, of course; and members become used to finding their way round a script, and to reading aloud – both skills which not everyone has at first, but need to be practised.

Libraries have sets of plays which may be borrowed on a long-term basis, and some publishers hold perusal copies and occasionally sets of plays, which groups or individuals may borrow. There are also playwrights who use a website to promote their work, and they, too, give an outline of the play, sometimes with permission to photocopy it once an initial script has been bought.

At first, it is best to begin by looking at one act plays, since because they are relatively short, there will still be time left for discussion after the reading. Should the chosen play be longer – two or three acts – then the organiser may wish to pick out salient points of the plot and précis other sections, so that some understanding of the play is possible in one evening, thus also allowing time for discussion. Members can then take the script home to read in full if they wish, and so reach a better understanding of the work. Précising is never really satisfactory because some of the author's intentions will be lost, and it is merely suggested here because sometimes groups find it difficult to sustain interest in a play read, but not watched, from one week to another. Having read the play, members should be encouraged to assess the merits of both plot and character and to recognise how good dialogue can help bring it all to life.

It is helpful to those listening, however, if the organiser or another member can read in, or better still précis, the stage directions. Listening to dialogue without seeing a player's moves can be confusing – even more so if parts are passed between readers during the action. If voices are to change during a reading, it is wise to have read the play first, so appropriate change-over points can be planned in advance.

An 'inclusion' policy should be used during play readings, as it should with any activity organised for members, with everyone being given the opportunity to read if they wish to, even if it is only a few pages of dialogue. But since unsure reading takes away from the enjoyment and understanding of a play, it is helpful if those who have been asked to read can see the script before the meeting. This means that even those who are not good at sight reading will have the opportunity of reading aloud in private before doing so in front of others. In time, everyone will become practised in verbal expression, in listening and in picking up cues – all essential in acting – and there should be no need for practice before hand.

Having discussed the merits of plot, characterisation and dialogue, members will gradually reach an understanding of the writer's craft and this will help inform them when they are searching for a 'good' script for use in production. It will also be of value if they ever try to write their own play.

Note that rehearsed readings of any play in front of an audience does need the permission of the playwright's agent before it can take place.

4 RULES & REGULATIONS

what this chapter covers...

In this chapter we look briefly at the *legal* considerations necessary before any play can be performed. These may influence the *choice of play*, so should be part of the play selection process.

COPYRIGHT

It is worth noting here the legal situation regarding the public performance of any play, even a rehearsed reading. You do need a licence to perform a play, even if you still have the script in your hand. Reading for private pleasure or for the education of any group does not require permission from the author's agent nor a licence, but you would need to acquire a licence if an audience, paying or not, is to be present.

The author of a play, or of any other published written work, holds the copyright to that work. Before anyone may perform it in public, they must have permission to do so and pay the required licence fee. Most authors have their agents deal with this, and so, before deciding on any production, and definitely before rehearsals begin, the group should obtain permission from the agent whose name is generally printed in the front of the play copy.

You should also note that adapting an original work or omitting text in a play amounts to a breach of copyright. Most agents issue licences on the understanding that 'the integrity of the author's work will be preserved'. However, if you do wish to 'cut' some of a play you may well find, on enquiring, that an author or his agent may be sympathetic to the request – it all depends on the writer.

Excerpts from written work also hold the same requirement for public performance, although if an excerpt is being used only for educational purposes (as in a workshop, for example) a fee should not be necessary.

You will not have to pay a licence fee if 70 years have elapsed since the author's death. This means that the original plays of writers like Shakespeare, Sheridan and Pinero (all full length and with large casts) will be out of copyright, and it is unlikely that payment of fees would be necessary. However, a fee may be payable if you use a newly published adaptation of the original work.

If you use a script which has been downloaded from the internet remember that you will have to pay a fee for performance as you would for any other play.

The wisest route if you are seriously considering the public performance of any play is to contact the agent before you begin work on it, for in some cases copyright has been extended.

ROYALTIES

This is the money paid to any author by his agent when a copy of his work is bought and of course this includes any dramatic work. It is against the law to photocopy scripts for use on a production. Scripts should be bought from the agent, and the costs become part of the budgeting for that show. In some cases those involved are asked to pay for their own scripts, which they will probably want to keep anyway.

VIDEO RECORDING

Most amateur groups would like to keep a record of their show for posterity, but the licence to perform does not include the right to record and most scripts state this categorically. You could seek permission from the agent to record a show for the archives, but even if permission is granted, and this is rare, you should not make multiple copies and they must not be sold to the public. The only exception both to this and the above rules would be if you had written the play yourself.

5 THINKING AHEAD

what this chapter covers...

Before beginning to put a production together, it is necessary to know exactly what your performance *venue* will be. In this chapter we consider the most common types of venue before going on to look at the various *business aspects* of planning a production. You will need to pay particular attention to *marketing* if your hard work is to be seen by as wide an audience as possible!

STAGING A PRODUCTION

As meetings continue and time moves on, you, as a group will doubtless begin to consider when you can begin to work on a production for public performance. You will decide what kind of play you wish to do and begin to look for a script which would be suitable for the company, but you'll also need to know where the production will take place. It's a fact that a performance may be staged anywhere where there is one area for the actors and another for the audience who come to see them, and you may decide that, since you already know your hall, you would like to perform a play there – but there is no stage. That doesn't matter, you could still go ahead, and create your first production in what is generally known as a Studio space.

STUDIO SPACE

Studio performances can be staged in any room as long as it is large enough to provide an acting area and seating for your audience. Audience numbers will be regulated by the fire regulations relating to the room, and you can arrange the acting area wherever it would be most appropriate in the light of where your audience would sit. Set design should be kept to a minimum, you may have to have to use screens to simulate entrances, and you couldn't have too large a cast. But since your audience is very close to you, on the same level, in fact, a Studio space creates an intimacy and a relationship between cast and audience which is not found in many other areas of theatre, for most plays performed by an amateur drama group take place on

An end stage. This means that the performance space is set at one end of a room, with the audience seated facing the stage. This may or may not be raised above the seating area, but if it is at the same level, as in an ordinary community hall, it may be necessary for the blocks of seats to be raised (raked) or staggered (see p48) so that members of the audience have a clear view of the action. Most halls, however, do have an end stage raised above floor level, and this is generally framed by a proscenium arch which faces the audience, separating them from the actors and 'framing' the action. This is the most commonly used design in theatres in England and the easiest stage for amateurs to act on, as well as being the one they most often use.

Other areas used for theatre are:

A thrust stage which sees the audience sit on three sides of the acting area – for examples see The Swan at Stratford upon Avon and the reproduction of Shakespeare's Globe Theatre in London. An amateur actor may not, at first, find this an easy area to work in, for he would have members of the audience at the side of him as well as in front – but it is unlikely that many amateur groups would have the opportunity of using such a stage for their first production.

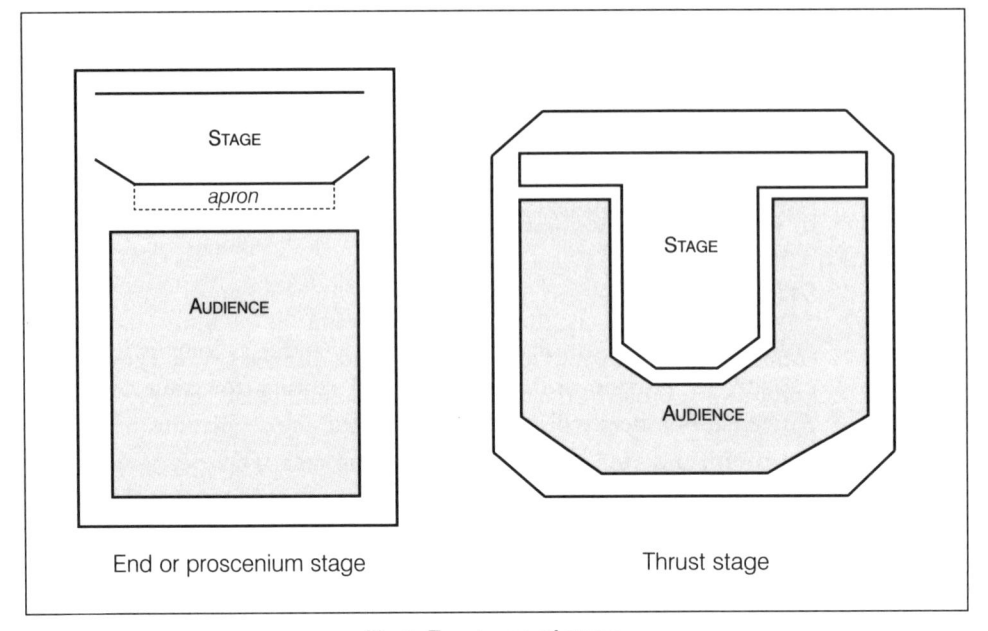

Fig 2. Two types of stage.

Theatre in the round where the audience completely encircles the acting area – as can be seen in the Stephen Joseph Theatre in Scarborough. The actors approach the stage by moving along aisles through the audience (or sometimes they may appear from under the stage) and at any given time they will therefore have their backs to one section of the audience. Again, an amateur group may find it difficult to work in a theatre of this design.

A Church

A group asked to perform within a church should consider carefully whether they would be able to do so. Now, theatre is rarely seen in a church, but it is the physical aspects of the buildings themselves which present most problems, and there are special rules regarding both the performance licence and health and safety matters. Conversation with the church authorities and/or the fire service would be useful to anyone contemplating church drama. As for the design of a church itself, the naves and the pulpit could be used to good effect but you may need a platform at one end which could act as a stage. This could prove costly since, in the interests of safety, you would have to ensure that it was well constructed. If the original pews were still there, seating your audience so that they had a clear view might be difficult too – although if the church had been modernised and the seating was removable, you may solve any staging problems quite easily. In fact, such a church might lend itself to the promenade style of theatre (see below). Lighting would have to be hired and costume carefully designed to suit the drama of the chosen play and its setting, and a high roof might cause problems with echo and audibility, unless much of the work was musical although some churches may already have a system of microphones and speakers installed at fixed points. But, having noted all that, any amateur group willing to take on the challenge of acting in a church would find it a very rewarding, if demanding, experience – but do look carefully at the area you would be working in before committing to the event. It is advisable, too, that the Church authorities know and approve of the content of your chosen play before you begin rehearsal.

Promenade

In the Promenade style of drama, actors working in different areas of the acting space perform each scene in order, often mixing with the audience, which moves to each group in turn. The scenes are generally played out on rostra so that the action is clearly seen, and both lighting and linking music, if well designed and in keeping with the subject, can be used to great effect.

STREET THEATRE

Street Theatre can be undertaken as a promenade event or played out in one agreed acting area in the High Street, using costume but a minimum of props – and you must arrange to keep these safely out of the way of souvenir hunters! You will, however, need to obtain permission for the event from the local police and it is advisable to make the request as early as possible before you hope to stage it. Street Theatre, which need not last very long and is best repeated several times during the hours you are there, is also a good way of advertising a production which you may be about to stage in the more usual hall or civic centre.

OPEN AIR THEATRE

Open Air Theatre can be quite exciting to perform, but is best undertaken by experienced actors. Without microphones good voice projection is very necessary, especially if a breeze is blowing away from the audience. The backdrop to the drama, which is often a Shakespeare play, would be scenic and pleasing, especially if it is within a large enclosed garden where you are less likely to be interrupted by passing children and dogs. However, it would be a challenge to a new company, and it might also prove to be a costly exercise. If there is no natural rise or specially designed outdoor amphitheatre (now found occasionally in modern city regeneration schemes) you would need to construct a safe stage, hire lighting, and a sound system. Wherever you work out of doors, do consider the seating arrangements for your audiences – do you provide it or do they bring their own – and be careful to position them so that the setting sun does not blind them during an evening performance. Work out what you're going to use as dressing room and wing space, if you need it, and make sure that you have an alternative indoor space if weather conditions go against you.

DRAMA FESTIVALS

Drama Festivals are another opportunity for members of any amateur drama group to gain experience before the public, and entrants have the added advantage of receiving an adjudication of the work they have presented. A Festival play does, however, have to be carefully timed, the set may have to be designed with travel in mind (to a venue perhaps unseen), and there will be work involved not only in liaising with the organisers but with the travel arrangements of both personnel and properties. An established company used to working on a production could take this in their stride, but a newly formed group may find the process, even for a one-act festival, is a little daunting until they have had some experience. The group should first balance the merits of entering a competition and receiving impartial, yet constructive comments on all aspects of their staging and performance, against the extra commitment of time and money that such a venture would bring. And one of the best ways of finding out whether this is something the group would like to do is, if it is at all possible, to go along to a drama festival as a member of the audience and see what happens!

As can be seen, there are many exciting possibilities for any drama company to consider, but many newly formed amateur groups decide that their first production will follow the more usual route of being staged in a hall or centre where there is an end stage, preferably with a proscenium arch, which will frame their endeavours and bring them success. A full breakdown of what is involved in the 'artistic' side of producing a show can be found on p53, but before that, it may be wise for the group to take into account all the other equally important business that is involved in staging a public performance within your community.

THE BUSINESS SIDE OF A PRODUCTION

Now the play and the venue have been chosen and you know how many people you can seat each night, you will, having taken into account the cost of the licence, have worked out roughly what your budget will be. This is the beginning of all the planning, without which your potential success could be a disaster, and this is when the non-acting members of your group will prove their worth. As the director, the actors and the backstage team begin work on the play, the 'business heads' will turn their mind to the local community, to work out how they can be persuaded to support the group, and also their needs when they become an audience. The work of these other members, perhaps forming a sub committee for the duration of this production, will be every bit as important as that being carried out during rehearsals, and plans for marketing can begin as soon as the play and the venue have been decided upon. After all, if there is no publicity, there may be no audience and although the company may reach the highest standard of artistic success, there will only be a few members of the community to appreciate it or share the group's enthusiasm for drama.

Ticket Pricing

Knowing the projected costs of your production, how popular you think the show will be and the seating capacity of the hall, will help guide you when it comes to deciding how much you should charge for tickets. To help the decision making, ask yourself

- What do other amateur drama groups in your area charge?
- How many nights are you playing for and how large an audience can you reasonably expect? It is better to underestimate the number of tickets you may sell rather than over estimate.
- How many concessionary tickets do you think you may sell – this includes children, the elderly, and in some areas the unwaged. This is a difficult question unless you live in a village area, for example, and are able to gauge for yourselves who may make up the majority of your audience. How many complimentary tickets (including the press if you invite them) will you have to discount when thinking of ticket sale numbers? Will you make a concession for block bookings? In many theatres this generally means one free ticket for every ten or twenty full price tickets paid for.

Decide from the beginning whether you intend to use credit card sales. These can incur extra expense and most amateur groups prefer to have cash or cheque sales.

The ticket price should reflect the value you place on your production and on the appeal of the play itself. Too low a price and you will undersell yourselves so that the public will think you are probably not very good; too high a price and some will not be able to afford to come or will compare you with prices in the professional theatre and decide to save their money for that! The best route to take is to do some research into what others locally are charging and then decide on the average. Inevitably you will learn from whatever decision you make this time and will be a little wiser next time around.

The Tickets

These can be designed and produced on a computer quite easily using light card. If you are only performing on two nights, they may be easier to collate if a different colour is used for each night. But whatever colour or design they may be, each ticket should contain the following information:

- The name of the group, the show, the playwright (along with any special note stipulated by the writer's agent) the venue, the date and time of performance.
- The ticket price in all categories- adult, child, concessions.
- A contact number and/or web site address

Unless you are working in a theatre, it is unlikely that the tickets will need to carry an allocated row and seat number for each seat. It is more usual for amateur shows produced in a hall to work on a 'first come, first served' basis when it comes to audience seating. If the ticket carries a number at all, it will be there simply as an aid for the organiser to help him keep track of how many tickets have been sold and who has sold them.

Ticket sales

If your show venue is a theatre or a civic hall with box office facilities the management there will probably be willing to handle both the ticket printing and the sales, but they will, of course, charge you commission for this work. It is a help to have this done for you and it will be efficiently handled, but it affects your budget, and so, for the purpose of advice offered in this book, we will assume that your new group will be performing in a small hall and that the ticketing will be your responsibility.

If there is no official box office, the task of selling tickets rests with group members, perhaps a local shop if the owner is willing to help, the telephone number of a member who may hold tickets for sale to anyone who does not live in the immediate area and perhaps the internet. Here the member responsible should agree to reserve requested tickets for a short time until payment has been received, when the tickets could then be forwarded to the payee (in which case, the cost of postage should be added on) or kept for collection at the door on the night of performance. Do set a date by which tickets reserved by phone or on line must be paid for, or you may find that you are left with tickets which you could have sold elsewhere. Selling through the members themselves has many pitfalls and experience shows that this can make for confusion and even to a loss of money. The following rules should help:

- One member should have total control of the tickets and of the moneys received for them. He should reserve any needed for known complimentary seats and if you are using a theatre, it is also wise to hold one or two seats as reserved or 'house seats', in case of confusion in the box office. These house seats can be sold at the last minute on the night of the performance.
- He should keep a list or a grid showing how many numbered tickets have been allocated to each individual member along with what those ticket numbers are. That member is then responsible for selling the tickets and returning payment for them by a set date preferably two weeks before the opening night.
- Members should not exchange tickets between themselves. 'Oh, I've got two left. You can have those if you need them', leads to confusion, and the organiser will lose track of where tickets are and who is responsible for returning the money they have earned. All unsold tickets should be returned to the organiser by the set date, and he can then mark them off as being returned, before re-allocating them to whoever needs more.
- The two week deadline will enable you to know how many seats you have left for those who may just arrive and hope to pay at the door. It is wiser, however, to sell all the tickets if you can. Anyone arriving without one cannot expect you to keep seats on the off chance that they may come, and they will realise that next time they must purchase their tickets in good time if they don't wish to be disappointed.
- When selling a ticket, the seller should ask if the purchaser will be using a wheelchair. If that is the case, a note should be made for the front of house manager to reserve a suitable seat or one of the allocated wheelchair spaces.
- The organiser should keep a watchful eye on ticket sales. If they appear to be faltering or are not up to expectation two or three weeks before the performance, press group members to try harder(!) and co-ordinate with the members responsible for publicity. It may also be worth investing in some extra form of advertising – recruit the local press if necessary.

If after that, the First Night bookings are still very poor, consider 'papering' part of the house for that one evening. This means that you give away tickets, generally by inviting groups of people to be your 'First Night guests', but do ensure that they will definitely come once they have been given a ticket. The owner of a retirement home, for example may have those who would like an organised outing to see a play, or there may be charity groups in the same situation. Timing here is important. Do this too early and you may lose real ticket sales. Leave it too late and the 'guest' groups may not be able to organise themselves in time. A full house on the first night means a good start to the production and more people to recommend it, which in turn will help to build an audience for subsequent nights.

Note. It is worth anticipating what the group will do if, for any reason, a performance has to be cancelled. If this does happen, you should be prepared to offer tickets for another night or refund the price of the ticket. If something happens to cancel the production altogether, you must immediately place a notice at the venue and in the press to this effect, with some explanation, notice of how any refunds can be obtained and an apology. This should be the very last resort if you are not to damage any good reputation you hope to build up. Remember 'the show must go on' no matter what the problem may be.

PUBLICITY AND MARKETING

THE POSTER

Whatever the size – and it is generally A4 or A3 – whether you are designing the show poster yourself on a computer, or having it done professionally, there are several things you should remember:

An advertising poster, whatever it is designed for, should be bright and eye-catching with the relevant information clear and concise. You may use colour in a pictorial design if you decide to use an image (although more than two colours can be expensive) or print on to coloured paper – though remember that black print on a red background is difficult to read, especially from a distance. Do what it takes to attract attention and then before you run off a large number for distribution, stand and look at it from a distance and see if you have been successful.

If you do incorporate an image of some kind, it should be clear, relevant to the theme of the play and perhaps intriguing enough to make people want to see the production. If at all possible, try to use an original image or drawing, for if you copy a design which has already been used, perhaps by a professional company, you may find that you have infringed copyright.

Make the layout of image and information balanced and pleasing to the eye, not an amateur jumble of words. The more professional your poster appears, the more confidence both you and the public will have in the production, for in everything your group does, high standards must be maintained if you are to be successful.

All the information should be clear enough for any member of the public to read and understand, even if they are passing in a hurry – although, hopefully, the poster itself will be attractive enough to persuade people to stop and read it. Make sure that you have included

- The name of the group presenting the show – and the word amateur should be included.
- The title of the play and the author's name, and if the agent demands that the playwright's name should be of a certain size or sit in a certain position with regard to the title (and occasionally this does happen), abide by the request.
- It is helpful to a potential audience if you give some indication as to the type of play it is – 'an uproarious comedy', 'an ingenious thriller', or perhaps take a phrase which describes it from the catalogue or the back of the script itself.
- If the play contains strong language or is unsuitable for children, you should state this on the poster. A member of the audience who may be offended then has no grounds for complaint. (The phrase 'for adults only' has been said to boost the audience numbers, but be sure that you are always only advertising what is true!)
- The dates and times of performance (and perhaps, if there's room, the time when doors open).
- Where the production is taking place.
- Give detail of the ticket prices, including concessions if there are any and where and how the tickets may be purchased.

Above all, do check all the text and spelling before the poster is reproduced. It's even better if two people carry out the check. One missed or misplaced letter or information left out, can mean double the expense if that mistake means that the initial print run must be scrapped and done again.

How many posters you reproduce depends on how widely scattered the play's potential audience may be, on how many places you can exhibit the posters and on the costs involved – although these will be

> **DANEMERE AMATEUR DRAMA GROUP**
>
> PRESENT
>
> # Murder in the Shrubbery
>
> by Alan Porter
>
> *a comic tale of blood, fish and bone amongst the roses*
>
> (CONTAINS SOME STRONG LANGUAGE)
>
> ## Wed 21st – Sat 24th Nov 2007
>
> at 7.30 in Danemere Village Hall
>
> Tickets available from Danemere Post Office or by phoning 01911 902314.
>
> £5 (£3 concessions)

reduced if you photocopy rather than print. If you are using a professional printing firm, have your agreement in writing, make sure that they have the posters ready at least a week before you need them for distribution, and build in enough time for that proof reading before they are actually printed off.

Distribution. Posters should be ready for distribution by the publicity committee and cast about eight weeks before first night, for they are the first intimation that the general public will have of the show to come. Don't assume that every business will agree to display your poster, although they are more likely to if you have been polite in your request. Remember too, that fly-posting is illegal, so you should not display them anywhere without permission.

If the play happens to be a set study book in secondary school, contact local schools with information, if not a poster or flier, three months ahead of the production. This is especially useful if you have hired a theatre space. In that case, you might enclose a letter to the Head of the English department, along with a booking form and details of prices for block bookings, suggesting that he may find it of benefit to the students if he were to bring a school party to one of the performances. If you hear nothing, you could repeat the exercise by sending another booking form and a flier six weeks before the production.

'FLIERS'

If the poster is clear enough, it may be reduced down to an A5 size leaflet and photocopied. Fliers are useful since they can be reproduced in larger numbers and used as a 'mail shot' through neighbours' doors, given to friends, or left in libraries, bookshops or in other places where people gather. This means that they may be easily picked up and used as a reminder by anyone who thinks this is a production they might like to see. It's possible, too, for members of the group dressed in suitable costume to walk round the town during a busy afternoon two weeks (or one if bookings are poor) before performance, handing leaflets to passers by – but check first with the police that this would not break any local rule.

Although the smaller size is not ideal as a poster, some shops may be more willing to accept this size for display, too. Individual Fliers can be distributed later than posters, for then they act as a reminder. Think how many times an advertisement is shown on the television. Repetition is important, but in the case of a local show, the repetition is perhaps more effective if the information comes in different formats – poster, flier, press and radio coverage. (See marketing p42.)

BANNERS

Occasionally some more established companies who are perhaps producing a musical or a prestigious play, display banners, and these are generally attached to buildings on either side of the high street so that they hang above the public in the local town. They can be expensive to produce and permission to use them has to be obtained from the local Council months, sometimes even a year ahead of the production date. A banner is unlikely to be used by a small local amateur group, and it is mentioned here simply as an additional idea.

Press release

Ideally, this should be written by the director, for he will know more about the show than anyone else, and then handed over to whoever is in charge of publicity/marketing. It should be short, to the point, perhaps with an eye-catching heading and a brief outline of the play (written without giving away any secrets) and any interesting points relating to it or the actors. It should also clearly state details which are on the poster − who is staging the production, when, where, ticket prices etc (see page 35). The release should also give the name and contact number of your publicity officer if you have one, or the director so that the journalist has a contact should he wish to know more. Mention can also be made if this is the company's first show, or give reference to the last one you did − especially if it was very successful!

The Programme

While thinking about a press release, the director might bear in mind that he may be asked to write a foreword or a welcome in the programme. Often, it is the responsibility of the stage manager to gather the information which goes to make up a programme, and in a local amateur group he will generally work with the director and whoever is in charge of publicity.

Layout will depend on how the programme is to be printed and to have it done professionally can be expensive. Better in the early days perhaps, to design it yourself on a computer, use a photocopier and A4 paper which can be folded in half, with, if possible, a reproduction of the poster on the front. The inside can then include a list of the cast and others who have worked on the show, along with information as to where and when the play is set, a list of the scenes and how long the interval will be. The back of the programme can acknowledge thanks for help (if there is no room on the inside pages) give notice of how to become a member of this happy group and, if applicable, information about the next production. If this is the type of simple programme you plan, its cost might perhaps be included in the ticket price and given free to the audience. Any theatre programme will show what should be included and in time, you may wish to have a programme which is professionally printed. To make that a viable proposition, you would need to encourage local businesses to advertise in the programme as a way of gaining revenue – and working to find and satisfy advertisers is a very time consuming job.

However your programme is prepared, do make sure that everyone's name is spelt correctly. To be sure, insist that everyone prints his own name as he wishes to see it (Stan or Stanley?) in the Stage Manager's lists. As with the poster, have two people proof read it before you print it off. It is best to leave the final photocopying to the last week as there may be many reasons why something may have to be changed or added at the last minute.

FURTHER ASPECTS OF MARKETING

There are several ways of marketing or promoting a production and if you approach those who may be interested in the right way, you will find that they are generally only too willing to help.

THE PRESS

Advertisements. These can be expensive, but are useful, especially in the last weeks before the show. You will have to decide, in the light of your budget, how many adverts you can afford, what size they should be and on which evenings it would be best to display them. The advertising department of your local paper will be able to advise you, but don't rely on paid advertisements alone, for the press can assist in other ways and you would not have to pay for that help.

Free entertainment guides. This column generally appears each week in the local paper, so a few weeks before the show ask for your production to be mentioned and make sure that the editor has the relevant information. Some libraries also produce free monthly 'What's On' guides which you could advertise in.

Articles/pictures. Six or eight weeks before the production dates, contact the journalist in charge of entertainment in your local newspaper, or whoever generally writes the drama reviews (if they are not named in print, ask the newspaper for their name) and tell them briefly about your forthcoming production. It is general now to use email, but there is a lot to be said for personal contact by telephone (or face to face locally), when you can better judge how much interest there is in what you are talking about and if you are going to have to work to encourage it – but try to keep the call brief. Follow up your conversation with a press release and a flier. During your initial conversation, ask if the paper would be willing to print an article, and have in mind an 'angle' which they may care to use.

It's especially useful if the 'story' you suggest would need a photograph. If you're doing a play which involves a car accident, for example, try to 'mock up' such a picture on waste land or in a car park – as in 'Something to Hide' by Leslie Sands; if your characters wear period clothes, set an appropriate scene with them in costume – King Henry VIII in all his glory near a local historic building, ('A Man for All Seasons' by Robert Bolt); if a tent is used during the play, arrange for a picture with your characters peeping out of it – ('Sisterly Feelings' by Alan Ayckbourn). There will always be something which will make an unusual, eye-catching, unexpected, perhaps even an 'out of season' picture (Christmas decorations in mid-summer?) but you will have to think of it, for the journalist will not know the play as well as you do. The fact that you have made your request early will give the journalist plenty of time to organise his work, although the best time for the article to appear in print would be during the last two weeks before production.

If you do receive help from any individual journalist, it is good public relations to ring or email to thank him for his help once the show is over. It doesn't take a minute, but such courtesy is appreciated and anyone who is thanked for his interest is more likely to help on another occasion, as long as the request doesn't come too often. It should be remembered that maintaining a good relationship with members of the public is always important.

Competitions. Sometimes a paper will work with you to set up a competition, and the multiple choice questions or word search or whatever it might be, are always so easy you'll wonder why everyone in the neighbourhood does not enter. You offer a prize – generally a pair of free tickets for the show, or two pairs if you can afford it – and later announce in the press who won them. Again, don't leave it too late to make the arrangements if you decide to use this form of marketing. Agreements made about a month before production for use in the last two weeks are most acceptable.

Reviews. This is the time too, to invite the journalist to come to see the play on the first or second night so that he may write a review of it – if you want him to. Again, make your request in good time. It won't boost your audience figures if the review appears on the last night because you didn't ask him to come early enough, and reporters who have this job can be particularly busy, especially during the pantomime season. Arrange to leave two complimentary tickets and a programme for him (two so that he may bring a friend) and a week before the first night ring to ask if he's still able to come so that you can organise a complimentary drink of his choice for the interval (a good way of reminding him of the agreement!) – and don't forget to do so!

Local Radio

Listings. Most local radio stations have a 'What's On' list, so do make use of this and send in the information requested well before the performance date – each station will have its own preference date, so contact them early and ask when that is. Your production should also be a newsworthy event in your area, so again, about a month before the production, contact the appropriate broadcaster with the press release. With this much notice, the station should be able to give you some air time, when the director may be asked to go in and talk about the show, or some members of the cast may be invited to record a snatch of the play for broadcasting.

Help! Is your company short of a prop, or an item of costume? If this is the case – or even if it isn't – broadcasting an appeal for whatever it may be is another way of creating interest in the production (and you can use this idea for the press, too). Generally, local listeners will be only too willing to offer help or to lend items. If they do, accept gratefully, take care of whatever it is and return it promptly after the show. If it is an item of major importance to the show, and if you can afford it, you may even offer a seat for the play, otherwise record your thanks to the individual in the programme.

The Internet

If one of your members can create a web site for the group, this could prove to be another useful marketing tool. Members of the press may use it to contact you, it will bring you to the notice of the public and to some of your potential audience, and you can give notice of future events.

It is even possible to incorporate facilities for ticket reservation and payment by credit card, but this is beyond the scope of this book. There are specialist manuals and on-line tutorials to help you with such matters should you feel it would be of benefit.

Production / Marketing Timetable

The time-table before production will vary, of course, depending on your circumstances. It's possible to work a month or two later than suggested, especially in the early stages, but it's better to have things ready too early than to be too late.

12 months	If you need or hope for sponsorship, look for it now, but you should have some idea of what the production will be.
6 months	check play availability, book venue and rehearsal space. Director may now begin planning with production team.
4 months	consider design for poster/fliers and calculate the number needed. check deadline dates for local entertainment guides.
3 months	audition and the beginning of rehearsals. contact members of audience based list if you have one; print posters/fliers. Update web site (if you have one) with news of show.
2 months	distribute posters, some fliers; print tickets; contact press and radio with press release and organise future publicity ideas with them.
6 weeks	arrange for programme printing if you're not doing it yourself.
4 weeks	organise newspaper advertising and contact the journalist again if necessary.
3 weeks	check ticket sales; check flier distribution again.
2 weeks	print programmes if they're 'in-house' if ticket sales are poor, call in press to help and 'push' members' sales.
1 week	remind anyone coming to review the show on first night.
First night	Meet and greet any special guests, sponsors, press and look after them, tonight or on whichever night they come.

After show – write or phone thanks to anyone who was especially helpful.

Fig 3. Suggested time scale for marketing your production

AUDIENCE-BASED MARKETING

This is something which may be considered by an amateur group once it is established, for it takes time and could prove costly (in postage if you don't use email), but if the group works within a small community, it may not be necessary anyway. All the same, since one should speculate to accumulate, it could be money well spent if your company is large and you use a town centre venue.

To create an audience base, you could, for example, slip a form into the programmes, asking members of the audience to tick boxes saying how they heard about the show, the type of show they enjoy most, any comment they may care to make and whether they would like advanced knowledge of your next production. If this is the case, they fill in their name with postal and email addresses. Provide a box for them to slip the form into as they leave.

Analysis of this simple form will give you an idea of what kind of drama is popular in your area, where your core audience comes from and how far people have travelled to support you, and, more importantly, you will have an address when you come to mail-shot publicity for your next show. Don't use the form filling idea too often, keep the questions brief, create a database of the information you receive and remember to use it. Alternatively, you could speak to audience members personally – which you probably will anyway – but you will never be able to speak to everyone.

FRONT OF HOUSE

FRONT OF HOUSE

The work which group members carry out Front of House – in the foyer, its surrounds and the auditorium or hall – is very important, and the **Front of House Manager** is the lynch pin of his team. Not only are these members the public face of your company, but it is they who are responsible for the safety and well being of your audience and for seeing that all legal requirements within the venue are met. They have much to do before the production takes place as well as during it. Since they are in direct contact with the public, they should be well dressed, courteous, welcoming and helpful at all times. Some groups identify the FoH personnel by a badge or sash, or by asking them to wear a certain colour (perhaps black and white). Whatever it is, it should be easy for a patron to identify them if he needs their assistance. The Manager especially should be an efficient organiser, capable of dealing with any emergency in a calm and reassuring manner.

The Front of House Manager

He it is who should:

- Be one of the first to arrive at the venue so that he can make sure that exterior and interior doors are unlocked, (although in fact it often happens that on First Night it is members of the backstage team who are generally the first to arrive).
- Make sure that the Fire doors are unlocked and the exits are clear while the building is in use. When everyone, (both audience and members of the group), have left the building at the end of the evening, he should ensure that all doors are locked again.
- Organise other members of the front of house staff – those who collect tickets at the door, show people to their seats and sell, or distribute, programmes, ensuring that they know what to do in the event of someone arriving late or without the ticket they have paid for. On their behalf, and before opening the doors to the public, he should also liaise with the treasurer so that the box office has a float of money and any spare tickets which can be sold, and that his programme sellers have a float too. All monies should be returned to him or to the treasurer after the performance, safely locked away and never left in the hall overnight.
- Make sure that his assistants know what to do in the event of illness or an accident to a member of the audience, and that they know the evacuation procedure should fire break out. Before the production dates, he should have obtained this information from the owner of the venue, especially with regard to where the gathering points are outside the building.
- Ensure that during each performance he knows where the First Aid box is, and that there is someone in attendance who has had training in First Aid. It could be a member of the group or you may have to invite a member of the St John's Ambulance organisation to sit in on the show, in which case, you may be charged a fee or asked for a voluntary contribution.
- Make sure that any show photographs and necessary notices are in place by the entrance door before the audience arrives. These may

be simply to the effect, for example, that taking photographs is not permitted, that late-comers may not be admitted until there is a scene change, or a warning that strobe lighting is used during the performance – all notices which are more likely to apply when working in a theatre.

If you are working in a hall or a community centre without fixed seating, the Manager (with some assistance) will be responsible for setting out the chairs so that they are ready for the audience at least ten minutes before the doors open to the public. If the floor is not raked, the chairs should be set in a staggered formation – ie the centre of each chair in one row should be set behind the end of a chair in the row in front, so that each audience member has a clearer view of the stage. The law now dictates that the chairs should be of the type which slot together in groups of no less than four, with enough distance from the row in front to allow for comfortable seating. It is now that the Manager should ensure that seats, which have been reserved for a guest or someone with special needs, have a notice to that effect set upon them.

If he has been informed that a wheelchair space is needed, he should leave a gap at the end of the allotted row of chairs, which is generally at the front.

He must check that the centre and side aisles comply with the 1 metre width requirement laid down in health and safety rules, and then before the public enters, he should check that the hall is neat and tidy before opening the doors.

Before the House lights can go down at the start of the show and after the interval, the Manager will liaise with the Stage Manager. Having made sure that all members of the audience are settled, and that there is no-one still at the box office, in the Bar, coffee room or toilets, he signals clearance to the SM, closes the doors and goes to his own allocated seat. At the interval and the end of the show, it is he who opens the doors for the audience to move out of the hall. If there are two entrances to the hall, he should arrange for one of his helpers to be responsible for one of these entrances.

When the audience and company have left the building at the end of the production, he (with the stage manager), should ensure that all areas are left tidy and that all notices and display photographs have been removed.

CLOAKROOM FACILITIES

It is wise to investigate these when you hire the venue, especially since you must know exactly what they are before you begin to market the show. Is there a toilet for the disabled? Is there a cloakroom where coats can be left, and is there a notice disclaiming liability should anything be stolen? Make sure there is one, otherwise your group, as the hirer, may be held liable should anything go missing.

REFRESHMENTS

Most people appreciate a drink during the interval and it is up to you what you serve. If there are kitchen facilities, it may be tea or coffee, soft drinks or ice cream and you should arrange for a team of members to organise this. What you charge should cover the costs of buying the coffee etc with a small surplus to go toward the general funds. Ice creams can be bought in bulk at a Cash and Carry, stored in someone's freezer and brought down to the venue in a freezer bag just before they are needed.

However, do bear in mind that if the kitchen is near the hall, the cups and saucers must be set up before the show begins, all washing up must be done during the interval or at the end of the show and anyone in the kitchen area during the actual performance must remain quiet. Neither actors nor audience would appreciate the rattle of crockery during the performance.

If you wish to sell alcohol, you must be sure that the owner of the venue has the appropriate licence, and should you be responsible for obtaining an occasional licence, you must apply to the local magistrate's court for it, well in advance of the production dates.

RAFFLE

This, as everyone knows, is an ideal way of boosting the funds (see p18). Display the prizes in a safe place, sell the tickets and then make a public draw during the interval or a private one during the second half of the show. If the audience is present when the draw is made, they can either collect the prize there and then or after the show. If the draw is done privately during the show, the winning tickets should be fixed to each prize and a large list of the winning numbers exhibited in the foyer, where everyone can see it as they leave. But whichever way the draw is made, do not sit at the back of the hall tearing the ticket stubs within hearing of the audience. Such ripping and rustling, along with the whispering of the ticket sellers which sometimes goes with it, can be infuriating to someone intent on the play, and it is unnecessary. All that is needed is some thought and consideration.

SECTION 2

SHOWTIME

6 PLANNING A PRODUCTION

what this chapter covers...

In this chapter we will consider the different *types of production* available to a drama group. These include plays, musicals, pageants and revues.

We will then look at the factors involved in deciding which type of production is most suitable when your *budget, venue, membership* and various other skills involved in staging a show are taken into account.

CHOICE OF PRODUCTION

Having shown that any drama production is very much a team effort, and that every member can make a valuable contribution to your success, it's time to decide what exactly your public is going to see. If you've had play reading evenings you may already know what you want to do, but for a new group about to launch itself into the public eye for the first time, here are some things to consider.

As a general rule, it is unwise for a new group to begin with a great musical extravaganza or a long three-act play, and not many would wish to do so, if for no other reason than both would involve a great deal of rehearsal. In fact you would probably prefer to rehearse one act plays, so that you have the satisfaction of seeing the finished product after only a few months work, without having to perfect, not only acting, but the equally specialist arts of music and dance. But whatever you plan to stage as your public performance, whether it's your first or fiftieth, do remember that the work involved must be shared among members of the group. Neither the leader nor the director can do it all on his own. So the secretary or treasurer could handle booking space and sending for scripts, for example, while other work – set, costume and properties – is divided between those who will not be acting this time. Also remember that even when you have chosen your play:

- You must obtain permission for its performance from the author or his agent before any rehearsals begin and you must budget for the licence fee which you will have to pay (see p27).

- You will also need to organise performance dates well in advance, at least six months in advance, both for rehearsals and for the venue you hope to perform in.

Bearing this in mind, and having considered what you think your potential audience would like to see, you can now decide exactly what you're going to do.

FOUR TYPES OF SHOW YOU MAY CONSIDER

DRAMA

As already noted, a new amateur drama company often prefers to begin with One Act plays. This makes line learning a less onerous task and the text doesn't generally require as much study as a full-length, two act play. A double bill of two one act plays can be popular, for they give the group more acting opportunities (although the director, unless he has an associate, has to work in two fields at once, as it were). However, try to link the plays through a theme if possible and choose those with simple sets or you'll overload your backstage workers.

MUSICAL

This is, in many respects, a very demanding genre for any drama group but especially for a new one, since it will require not only a producer and a cast with singing/dancing talent, but also musicians, a musical director and a choreographer.

PAGEANT

This could be a true, 'in-house' production if there are those in the group who know some of the history of the local area or are able to research material for a particular anniversary – as many did in the millennium year – and are able to formulate a script. But this would involve research and improvisation, with the inclusion of suitable music and perhaps dance, and it would take some time to come to fruition. So although it could be a very rewarding project in which everyone in the group could take part, it may be wiser, at this stage, for a new company to choose for their first venture, a script which has already been tried and tested and which will not take a very long time to rehearse.

REVUE

The term 'revue' here includes a Variety Show or perhaps a Music Hall. A Revue may be a good first production for a new group, especially if the items can be linked by a theme, such as Spring-time, Christmas, Love and Marriage, Battle of the Sexes or an anniversary. A Revue has the advantage of producing variety within a show (so there should be something to please everyone in the audience!) and it gives members with different artistic talents a chance to show what they can do. You will, however, need an experienced director who's able to link the items together cohesively, and the performance should be well dressed and very well rehearsed.

If this is to be your choice, make sure you have members who are able to show off a party piece, and others who can play the piano, sing or dance, or have a talent for stand-up comedy. There should be someone who would be willing to perform a monologue or who can read verse or prose well. Add to these talents a few sketches or a mime, a Chairman to introduce the acts, and you've not only created a revue, but have given members the opportunity of getting up on stage, perhaps for the first time. Once they've appeared on a stage together, even if it's only to perform a short item, they'll know they can do it and will have the confidence to begin work on that full production which you've decided is to be the next goal. Do remember, however, that whatever you do, you'll have to obey the rules of copyright.

Some groups successfully combine their very first entertainment, a One Act play or a Revue perhaps, with fund-raising. It's possible to start the evening with a Bring and Buy sale and a raffle followed by light refreshments before the entertainment begins. Under these circumstances a Revue needn't be very long. The evening ends with notice of another, full production to come within a given time, generally six months. This way the group has been launched, advertised itself as being active, gained a potential audience who'll want to come to see what they do next, and hopefully made a little money to start the funds which they're going to need – and all without too much effort.

CONSIDERING A PLAY

Whatever the new project is to be, however, think it through before you buy a full set of scripts. For the purposes of this book, and assuming that the project will be a group's first attempt at producing a full evening's entertainment, we'll assume that the type of presentation envisaged will be that which is most common – namely, a play. Whether it has one act or two, there are the same points to consider if you're to make an informed choice. It may appear a long list, but if you've covered every angle, nothing should go wrong. So, add the following to your considerations when someone suggests a title or you start reading scripts:

THE MEMBERS

- what is the ratio of men to women among the members who wish to act?
- what is their age range?
- how many have had some experience as actors?

It would not, after all, be in your best interests to choose a play with a cast of twenty-year olds if all the members are over fifty, and conversely, it's not easy for very young actors to play elderly people, even with make up. It's better, especially with your first production, to choose one with characters who more or less reflect the age range and sex of the acting membership.

If one of the parts in the play is demanding either in characterisation or line learning, then you should cast the more experienced actor in this role (providing that he/she would be physically suitable) so that that actor becomes the cast's lynch pin and role model. The knowledge and confidence he should bring to the part will help any newcomer for, as in sport, one can learn much from the example of an experienced player.

Since this will be the first time an audience will see your work, acting must be of the highest possible standard, otherwise people may be unwilling to return for your next show. That's not to say, of course, that only those with experience should be allowed to audition. No-one will ever learn if they're never given the chance and the least assuming member often proves to be one of the best actors.

THE PLAY

Play-reading evenings often help when choosing your production. As well as library collections, there are play publishers who produce catalogues giving details of the plays they hold – details of cast and set requirements, the period in which the play's set and the plot – all things to consider when choosing a script. Some agencies, too, are willing to supply perusal copies for a small fee and some web sites give detail of the plays they have and will also provide one copy, which in some cases may be photocopied. If everyone shares the task of looking for a suitable play the producer won't have to search around for one on his own, for it's a time consuming exercise. In the end, however, it is he who must have the final choice. He'll spend more time working with that script than anyone else and no-one can stage a successful production unless they like the play they're doing

But what kind of play do you wish to do – comedy, tragedy, murder, mystery, melodrama, farce or serious social drama? Which would you most enjoy doing and which do you think your potential audience would most appreciate? It's no use working on Shakespeare if you live in a community which wouldn't want to see it; melodrama demands a type of exaggerated language and movement; and, for an inexperienced group, farce is not as easy as it looks because it needs split second timing. Many amateur companies like to start with comedy if only because the play makes them laugh and they know they'll have fun working on it – and audiences, too, enjoy an evening out which leaves them feeling happy.

Above all, any group, new or experienced, should aim to find a *good* play, one which is well written, with a well constructed plot and some kind of conflict which will provide the drama or the laughs. It should be a play which moves along and carries its audience with it, with well-drawn, interesting characters and convincing dialogue – preferably without a dialect which would be unfamiliar to group members. If the characters are the kind of people whom inexperienced actors can identify with, so much the better. Beware of attempting an unpublished play written by anyone who hasn't had stage experience. In all probability experienced players could stage it successfully, but a new group would be much wiser to work on a script which has been honed and worked on so that any faults in writing, plot or character have been eradicated. It is worth paying for the licence when you know that you have a script which has been proven to work successfully.

It's essential, too, when finalising the choice of play, that you know if there are any members who, for one reason or another, won't be able to take on commitment for the proposed production dates or for the rehearsal weeks leading up to them. Every director, when considering a script, needs to know in advance just how many actors he can call on. It's possible to work round holidays but it makes extra work when trying to design the rehearsal schedule, and having someone absent in rehearsal makes it difficult for the others. Acting is, after all, a team venture.

The Venue

Another point you must bear in mind is the venue you're finally going to perform in, and in particular, what the stage is like. It is no good choosing a play with a cast of thousands or a complicated set if the stage is small and cramped, or you couldn't afford the money or the manpower to build the set needed, even supposing the stage were big enough. So you should know where the show is to be staged before you make the final choice of play. If you're not actually going to use a stage, you must know the size of the area you'll be working in and what its immediate surrounding are like, along with detail as to changing facilities and where exactly you can expect your audience to be. Even if you're applying to do street theatre, there will be areas where you'll not be expected to go. If your production is to be in the room you generally work in, then you'll already know

- How big the stage is (assuming there is one)
- How many entrances there are and where they're positioned
- How big the wing space is
- If there'll be room to store your furniture and props overnight
- Where the dressing rooms are in relation to the stage
- Whether there's a lighting and/or sound system which you'll be able to use

These are all questions you need to ask wherever you'll be performing.

However, should you have to hire a hall other than the one you generally use, you'll also need to know

- The dates the venue will be available
- Its seating capacity
- The cost of hiring the venue – in fact, many of the questions you had to ask when you first looked for a regular meeting place. Ensure, too, that the hall is licensed for the kind of public performance you'll be staging.

When you've found the venue, even if you're not yet sure of your choice of play, pencil in the performance dates with the booking secretary as soon as you can, with at least two other evenings (immediately before First Night if possible), ready to be confirmed when a definite decision has been made to go ahead. This applies whether it's for your regular meeting hall or whether it's to be an outside venue. You'll need the two extra nights for final rehearsals on the stage you'll be using, so that you have time to put up the set, and adjust any lighting and sound if applicable, and also so that the cast have time to familiarise themselves with the stage, its exits and entrances and their changing areas, before First Night.

THE SET

Look at the set design in the play you're considering. Is it complicated, would you be able to replicate it, or is the play one which would be equally successful if played in a simpler set? The design shown at the back of the script is generally that used when the play was first performed by a professional company and if it's large or complicated, it's unlikely that an amateur group would have the time or the expertise to build that design, or have the money to fund it. Then, too, the play may demand an upstage entrance, which your stage may not have (unless the actors are prepared to crash through the back wall) but there are ways round such problems. With imagination and some ingenuity, it's possible to re-design a set for the play you want to do, a design which will satisfy the demands you must make on it and one which will fit the stage you'll be working on. So don't dismiss a possible play out of hand if the set looks difficult. Most directors, anyway, like to put their own stamp on a production by re-designing it, if only marginally, to suit their interpretation of the play. More information on this and on set dressing can be found on p69.

COSTUME

Is the play very demanding as regards costume or would you be able to dress the actors without too much expense? Costume drama is popular with audiences and makes for interesting playing for the actor, but since they are both difficult and expensive to make, period clothes generally have to be hired (see p71).

AVAILABILITY

Once you think you've decided on a play, you should ask the agency which holds the rights to it whether it will be available for performance by amateurs at the time you hope to stage it. Their telephone number will be in their catalogue of published plays, or inside the play copy. The agency will tell you if it's a play that may only be performed by professional companies, which does sometimes happen, and the cost of the licence you'll require if you perform it. Once you have definitely decided to go ahead, you must formally apply for permission and pay the sum demanded when requested. It's worth noting that you should inform the agency of the size of your venue, for if it will only seat a small number of people, the licence to be paid may not be as high as it would be for a 200 or 300 seat auditorium. As has already been noted, a playwright holds the copyright for his work, this extends for 70 years after his death, and it's a criminal offence to present a play before the paying public without a licence. Sometimes agents do check this has been obtained, and although you may hear of companies who 'forget' to apply, it's really not worth risking facing legal action, thinking it wouldn't matter, perhaps, because it's only a one-act play.

Your Budget

As part of this decision making, it's important that you have in mind a budget. Estimate what you think the production is going to cost in hall rental (including rental for rehearsal time), script royalties, licence, costume, set building or painting, and possible hire of transport for furniture and scenery if you don't have a large enough van. Set aside a sum for 'extras' – properties, for example, or the printing of posters, programmes and tickets, if you can't do them yourself. Balance this against your projected income, from ticket sales, having decided on a reasonable ticket price, what you may make on programmes (if anything), refreshments, if you can serve them, and any sponsorship you may have been fortunate enough to acquire. Having checked your figures, you may find that perhaps you may not be able to stage that large cast, expensively dressed play just yet after all. Perhaps the group should wait a little longer for that pleasure and begin with a simpler production this time – a production which will be no less effective, but will leave you with a profit. The decision is yours!

The Decision!

Finally, now that the figures have balanced and everyone in the group has read the available play and agreed on it, you should confirm your booking at the performance venue for the dates which were pencilled in when you made your initial enquiry. Then, make sure you have enough copies of the script – one for each speaking part with five or six extra copies (for the stage manager, prompt, the set designer/builder, whoever is in charge of props and costume and the sound and lighting operators if you have them). Now you're ready to take the next, and most exciting, step – that of bringing to life the printed word for the enjoyment of both yourselves and your audience!

7 THEATRE-SPEAK

what this chapter covers...

Theatre uses words and phrases which can puzzle anyone new to the stage, so it is as well to know the 'technical' terms before you come across them in a script or hear them from someone used to drama. In this chapter we look at some of those most commonly encountered.

TECHNICAL TERMS

Stage Left, Stage Right. This always means left and right from the actor's point of view, so, for example, an actor obeying script instructions to move left will, from the audience point of view, be moving to the right across the stage. Upstage and downstage is fairly obvious – upstage being, to the actor, up and away from the audience, and downstage being down towards the audience.

Apron. The forestage area of a stage in front of the curtains and the proscenium arch.

Wings. This area, hidden from audience view by flats or curtains, lies immediately to the left and right of the stage. Here properties will be laid ready for use and here actors wait and shiver until they must appear on stage. It may or may not be lit by a low-powered blue light to avoid accidents. It's worth remembering that any sound made in this area will almost certainly be heard in the hall.

The Prompt corner. Generally in the wings, downstage left, where a small space may be set aside for the prompter, who, often with torch in hand, will pore over the script, while praying that the actors don't forget their words. In a professional theatre, this is generally situated in front of the Desk. Here, the Deputy Stage Manager sits with script and headphones which link to the technical gallery. There technicians await their cues which will tell them when to change lighting states or bring in sound. In amateur drama, the prompter will sit wherever he or she is able to see the actors, while at the same time being out of view of the audience.

The Tunnel. Not a word often used in amateur drama unless you're fortunate enough to work in a theatre or hall which has a passage way immediately behind the back of the stage, a corridor which leads from stage left to stage right. This 'tunnel' enables actors to enter from either side of the stage, irrespective of which side they exited from or where the dressing rooms may be. Without the tunnel, unless he runs through the rain to re-enter the building on the other side (and this can sometimes be necessary in a small hall!) the actor will have to return on stage on the same side as that from which he made his exit.

Flats. The name for the sections of scenery placed along the back and/or sides of the stage as a background to the action. They're made of a framework of timber or light steel across which is stretched muslin canvas, calico or sometimes plywood, surfaces which can be painted to represent the appropriate scenery. Flats can be between one and six feet wide and eight, 12, 14 or 16 feet high. They are linked together and then firmly braced and supported at the back by weights. For an amateur company in a hall, the existing walls or curtains can provide an

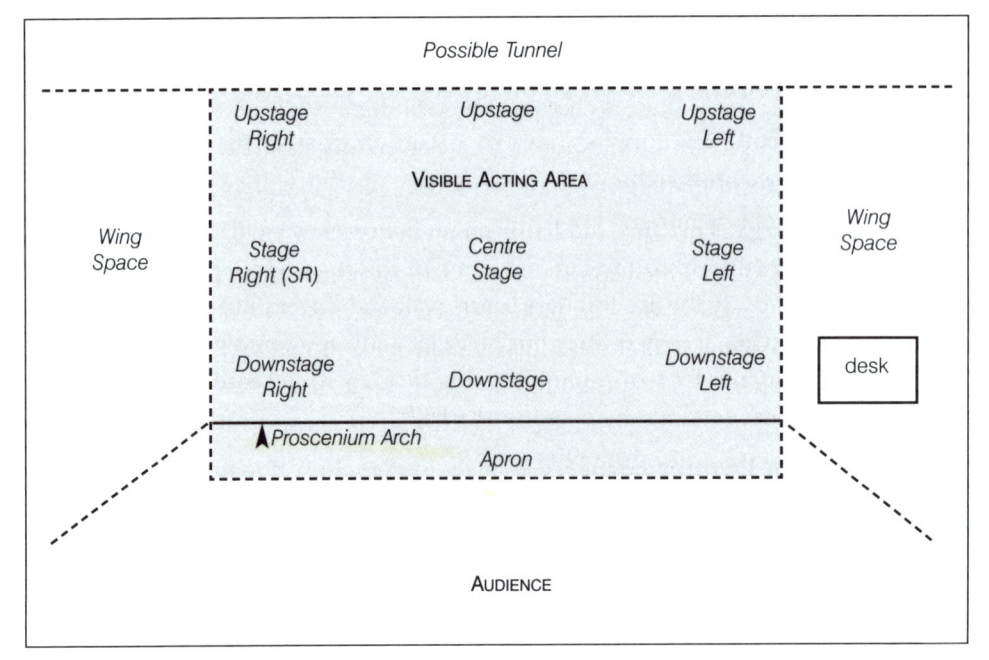

Fig 4. Parts of the stage.

adequate background for a play. Curtains which can be hung separately, especially at the sides along the wing space, are useful in that they will provide openings for entrances and exits. In the theatre these side curtains, often narrow and black and able to be hung at an angle if necessary, are sometimes known as 'legs'.

Cyclorama, often called the 'cyc' is the back wall of a stage behind a curtain or flats. When painted a light colour, it can, with the correct lighting, be given a projected background, such as sky, rather than having to use a painted backcloth or flats.

Raked. Some stages, especially those in a theatre are raked, which means they slope down slightly from the back to the front, as indeed do seats in an auditorium. Unfortunately this is not the case in most halls, so if that's to be your venue, positioning of the furniture both on stage and in the hall itself is very important if members of the audience sitting at the back are to have as clear a view of the stage as possible. To this end, the hall chairs are generally staggered. On stage, it's best to avoid placing heavy furniture with a high back at the front of the stage, since when actors walk behind it, the audience can only see them from the waist up – or less if they're small!

FX. The cue for the sound (effects) technician. Each cue is numbered.

LX. The cue for the lighting technician – again, each cue has a number.

Blocking. This is when the director instructs the actors on the moves he wishes them to make. He will have worked them out before rehearsal, but they're not set in stone. Actors should note these in their scripts in pencil, for if a move doesn't work it will need to be changed ie. rubbed out and rewritten.

Masking. This happens when one actor moves or stands in front of another, blocking the audience's view of him. As a fleeting movement it wouldn't matter too much, but an actor should take care not to mask another who is speaking. The word 'mask' also refers to the drapes or flats at the side of the stage, which prevent an audience seeing into the off-stage area of the wings.

Upstaging. An unforgivable sin, unless it's previously plotted as part of the scene. Upstaging happens, almost literally, when one actor who is placed upstage of others, takes attention away from the action or speech of other characters by too much movement or sound (or even by making a face!). By doing this, he becomes the centre of an audience's attention rather than his fellow actors who are, at that moment, an integral part of the play's action.

Get in or **Set up**. Exactly what it suggests, the time when you go on stage and prepare the set for performance. This work is generally organised by the production team and carried out by the backstage crew, although all helpers are welcome, especially in amateur drama, as long as they don't get in the way!

The Strike or **Get out.** This is the name for the time directly after the curtain has come down on the final performance, when the production team comes in to dismantle, in no time at all, it seems, the set which the actors have come to know and love! On this occasion everyone should be encouraged to help by doing what the crew ask of them, for many hands make light work and the sooner the stage is cleared and everything is stored or removed from the building, the sooner the group can celebrate their success in the Bar.

8 SETTING THE SCENE

what this chapter covers...

There's a lot more to a great production than just good acting! In this chapter we will look at the army of *back-stage* workers who create the world in which the actors perform. This vital group, from the *director* to the *production manager*, from the *sound designer* to the *property master* has an essential – if often seemingly invisible – hand in every successful show.

PRODUCTION PROFILES

WHO'S IN CHARGE?

It will be the **Producer** and/or the **Director** who will have the casting vote when the decision was made to choose a specific play, and in many cases in amateur drama that is one and the same person. In the professional world, the Producer (with his production manager) is generally responsible for the finance and over-all organisation of a production, for controlling spaces, stage, set and budgeting, and for assembling the crew, technical and backstage workers. The Director works to bring the production to life through his actors and the effects he's asked of the technicians. Since we are here dealing with amateur drama, the leader of the project could be referred to either as producer or director, for although he will principally be 'directing the traffic' on stage, he'll also be working with others, budgeting, planning and designing the production, as well as organising and overseeing those in the team responsible for everything else, from finding furniture or properties to dressing the actors or painting and dressing the set.

The producer of amateur theatre must be prepared to take on responsibility for the production and for everyone who'll work on it, listening and responding to them, encouraging and helping them to succeed. He it is who will ultimately be responsible for the overall artistic achievement of the work which the audience will see. He must have the ability to plan ahead and to communicate clearly with others, and he must be able to instill the discipline which theatre demands firmly, patiently and in a pleasant manner. Above all, he should always remain positive in the face of whatever may happen (and it often does!) It's not always an easy job, but it's a rewarding one. Ask any director as he stands at the back of the hall, watching the audience enjoying a performance of the production which he and his team have created.

THE PRODUCTION TEAM

SETTING THE SCENE

Quite clearly, the director and his actors can't stage a production on their own, a fact not always fully appreciated by the audience, nor sometimes even by the actors themselves. A great deal of preparation and sheer hard work goes into presenting any show before the public. In the professional theatre there are people with designated roles to do this work, but in an amateur company anyone and everyone must be expected to lend a hand, unless it's a really specialised task. If those who have been in one play take their turn doing backstage work for the next production, they'll soon appreciate just how much actors depend on the 'other half' of the team. You can learn a great deal about theatre if you do things other than act.

The following is a list of job profiles, loosely based on those in the professional theatre, which may help form an outline for a 'who does what' list for an amateur group about to stage a production for the first time, although in many cases, one person may undertake the responsibilities for more than one job. It's also helpful if two members can work together, job sharing, so that they can arrange a rota system of attendance during rehearsals. This can halve the work, it ensures that there's always someone there from whichever department, and more members will be involved in the production.

Before and throughout the project, the production team provides, services, supports and monitors the area in which the actors work. Between them they, with the Director, will design, build and dress the set, enhance it with light and sound, dress the actors, give them properties to work with and make sure that everything runs smoothly.

All these departments work together with the director's original concept to create a unity of setting, mood and atmosphere for the play,

Setting the Scene

Set Designer

1. To create a visual representation of the environment in which the action takes place, while encompassing the spirit and mood of the play.
2. To ensure that this is practical, safe, easy for performers to use and within the specified budget.

Lighting Designer

1. To illuminate both set and performers effectively, while creating a sense of time and place.
2. To use strength, direction and colour to enhance the play's mood and emotional content, both over-all and in any particular scene or area.

Director — **THE PLAY** — **Production Manager**

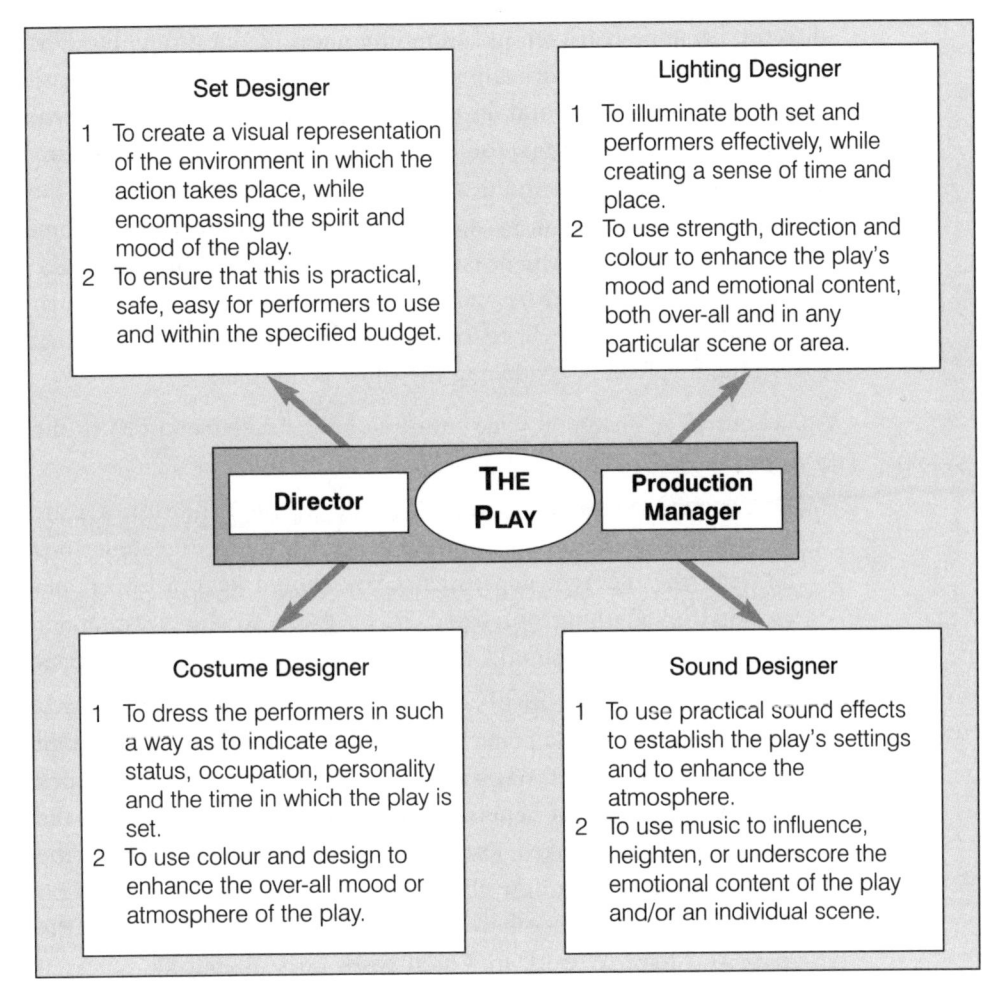

Costume Designer

1. To dress the performers in such a way as to indicate age, status, occupation, personality and the time in which the play is set.
2. To use colour and design to enhance the over-all mood or atmosphere of the play.

Sound Designer

1. To use practical sound effects to establish the play's settings and to enhance the atmosphere.
2. To use music to influence, heighten, or underscore the emotional content of the play and/or an individual scene.

Fig 5. The Production Team: How the Departments Link Together

each one being careful to complement the other, while at the same time taking into account the project's practical demands and its budget. They generally begin work many months before rehearsals begin, and at first a great deal of time can be spent in discussion and research of one kind or another. They must consider the play itself, the manpower, time and space available for executing the designs, the performance venue and the technical facilities it offers. Then, when final decisions have been made, their practical work begins.

THE PRODUCTION MANAGER (PM)

This is a designated job in the professional theatre, but in a small amateur company his work will probably be divided between the director, his stage manager and other members of the group. The PM is responsible for the 'non-acting' side of a production, overseeing all that this involves. He works in tandem with the stage manager (SM) and reports back to the director. Listing his duties here will remind any amateur company that there must be someone in charge of the 'production' side of the show; someone who, with others to help him (his crew) can take on these responsibilities, leaving the Director free to concentrate on his actors and the play itself. Through regular production meetings they'll co-ordinate their work and make sure that everything involved in producing the show is on track.

So, whoever's in charge in your company, be it a designated PM or the SM, you should, having read the play:

- Discuss with the director, designer (if there is one) and treasurer the costs of staging the production, and divide the budget for these costs between the different departments. You should keep a list of, and receipts for anything purchased, to be given to the treasurer for reimbursement, and should also keep watch on what's being spent throughout the production.

- Work with the director, (and designer if there is one), on the design and lay-out of the set, oversee all the practical aspects of the work on it (the purchase of materials and construction) and organise the 'get in' and the 'strike'. Just where the set will be built or the backcloths painted or how elaborate the set may be, will depend on the skills of group members (or their friends and family) and the space you have to work in. Often work goes on outside rehearsal time in garages or sheds. It's possible to work at the same time as rehearsals if you can use another room, but in this case great care should be taken to see that working areas are covered, and they should be left clean and tidy and not covered in dust or spattered with paint.

- Ensure that all parts of the set are safe, especially if using ramps, extensions or any other staging which has been specially built. If there is furniture (a chair perhaps) placed on top of extra staging, make sure that it's securely fixed. Ensure that any supports or weights used in the wings or backstage area are safely erected and clearly marked so that they may be easily seen by everyone backstage. You, as PM, with the Stage Manager, must also make sure that members of the crew carry heavy items with care, so that no-one suffers any injury while working on the show.

- Appoint other members of the group to be in charge of the various departments – stage management, costume, properties – and assist them whenever necessary.
- Organise regular production meetings with them and the director, the first being before rehearsals begin, so that heads of departments know what their responsibilities are. Thereafter you should meet with them periodically so that you can be sure that everything's running smoothly, and can help solve any problems which may arise.
- When the performance venue is different from the space where rehearsals are held, you will be responsible for arranging transport, if needed, to deliver and return furniture etc between the venues.
- With the stage manager, you should ensure that the performance venue is always left secure and in a clean and tidy state.

SET DESIGNER

An amateur company with someone experienced in stage design is fortunate indeed. Generally, the director will know what he wants but may be unsure how to achieve it and his initial ideas may have to be simplified, not only because of the space he'll be working in, but also on the grounds of cost.

Many plays, especially domestic dramas, are played in a **box set**, where the back wall of the stage and the wings form three sides of a room, with the audience being the fourth wall. But whatever the setting of the play, it's the designer's job, working closely with the director, to draw out (to scale if possible) a design of what's to be on stage, complete with measurements and details of the fittings and furniture needed. Here 'furniture' is used in its widest sense and includes anything which is needed to create the illusion of the setting, whether it be the interior of a drawing room or a hospital ward, a street scene or a forest, a garden or a split set encompassing two separate acting areas. The designer will also note down suggestions for colour and furnishings, which he'll finally agree with the director. If he can produce a model of the set, it will be a great help to everyone.

On the next page is an example of a simple set design drawing. Note that such a drawing may also be used by the Stage Manager (see p87) to check that all the furniture is correctly placed before each performance. The Stage Manager may also add in details of any essential props which need to be positioned and checked.

The designer then works with the production manager, or whoever's in charge of creating the set. In an amateur company, this work could include selecting and painting flats, but it's more likely to entail gathering together curtains, furniture and furnishings, possibly building an extra rostrum or platform of a different height as an effective on-stage acting area if it's required, or designing and painting scenic backcloths. Most small amateur companies don't have the luxury of a set designer or of items like flats – nor the space to use the latter if they had. However, with ingenuity and imagination, it's still possible to create a set which will be convincing as well as pleasing to the eye, and not too difficult to construct. For example, if a window is needed on a back wall and clearly there's not one there, it's easy to hang a drawn blind or a set of curtains on a wire or pole which can be set across a bar or hooks at the required height. Any 'view', if it must be remarked on by an actor, is hidden behind a net between the curtain drapes. This will be 'seen' by the actor as he carefully lifts aside a corner of the blind or the net. If there must be a view, then a painted backcloth hung behind the window frame and/or curtains will be necessary. As will be seen when we consider the role of the property master or mistress, in amateur drama necessity is truly the mother of invention!

One added note of caution here: whatever you use as furnishing on stage should be either of a non-flammable material or treated with a flame retardant spray. If in doubt, consult with your local fire officer.

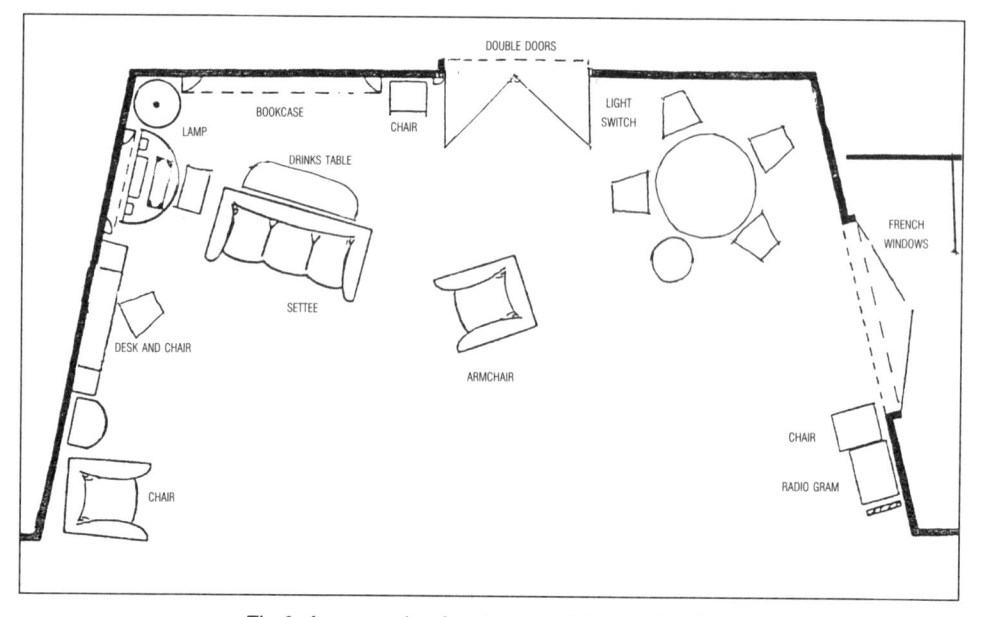

Fig 6. An example of a simple set design drawing.

Wardrobe Mistress

Having read the play, and talked to the director and the designer, if there is one, the person in charge of costume will have some idea what she should be looking for — this work generally falls to a woman. Some amateur groups are fortunate in already having a small costume wardrobe, but generally when it comes to dressing the actors, it will be necessary to make, beg, borrow or hire what's required. It's hoped that the director will have borne this in mind when choosing the play, for making an Elizabethan dress, for example, is not easy, hiring can be an expensive business and even clothes which were fashionable only a few decades ago are not always easy to find. However, charity shops can often be a treasure trove and if you're fortunate enough to have an inventive wardrobe mistress who can sew, no problem should be insurmountable. It will, though, be a great advantage if she can have someone to help her share the work both before and during the production. So, if you are to be the wardrobe mistress, you will need to:

- **Consider the budget.** Make sure that you know what your budget is. It's best to try to work below the given figure, for inevitably there will be last minute items, trimmings etc, which will take you over budget if you haven't made provision for this in the beginning.
- **Measure the actors** and keep a record of their measurements for future use. Make a list of costumes for scene.
- **Be aware of colour.** Take into account when choosing colour, the background against which the actor will be seen, although this is something which should have come up in discussion with the director/designer. If care isn't taken in the early stages to decide on a colour scheme, you may find that the girl in the red dress clashes, or even virtually disappears when she sits on a crimson sofa. Vivid colours show up well against a neutral background and deep, rich costumes are effective against a bright background. Pale pastel colours can fade to nothing under stage lighting.

  Remember that colour is important when matching character to costume. The shy girl is unlikely to wear bright, clashing colours, and harmony of colour on stage can do much to create the required atmosphere for any play. Bright orange, yellows or reds could shatter the mood in a serious play about retirement or death, for example, while young actors starring in a comedy wouldn't be so convincing in muted greys, browns or sepia. Limiting a range of colour can be

Re Wardrobe/costume p16 printout.

	Size	height	chest	waist	hips	collar	ins.leg	shoes	
Diane *Lady P.*	14	5'7"	38	32	38	--	--	7	grey dress, chifn soft shoes, grey
Iain *Clay*		5'10"	44	44	42	17	32	10	hackg jacket, bn slacks, check sht
Pat *Posey*	12/14	5'2"	36	26	36	--	--	5	pale grn dress, scarf, sandals
Philip *Arthur*		6'	40	34	34	15½	33	9	Flannels, sht wt o/n, navy blazer
Jim *Nick*		5'9"	40	38		15	30	10	blue sht, bl trs cap, wellies
May *Heidi*	12	5'4"	32	26	34	--	--	5	black dress as before

Fig 7. The essential 'specifications' of each member of the cast.

very effective too, for it can underline or harmonise all aspects of the play and/or its subject. A production of the life of Sir Thomas More in 'A Man for All Seasons', for example, looks most effective if, since these events take place in the latter years of More's life, the cast are in a combination of autumn colours, (rust and browns, greens, yellows and grey) with only King Henry VIII wearing a brighter, vibrant costume, cream perhaps, with trimmings of gold. A striking and dramatic effect can be achieved if a play is staged only in black and white, but this can only be done with certain plays and it would, of course, be the director's decision.

- **Consider accessories.** Make sure that these are in keeping with the period and shoes, especially, should be of the right design if at all possible. Libraries often hold illustrated books on costume, which can be a great help. It's not always possible, of course, to be exact, but always try to be as true to the period as possible. If a play demands that actors wear unfamiliar shoes, ensure that they have them to rehearse in over a period of time. If the ladies are to wear long skirts, arrange for them to wear their costume during the latter stages of rehearsal, or suggest that they rehearse in a long skirt of their own. Period dress affects the wearer's posture and movement.
- **Be responsible for wigs.** Hire wigs if these are necessary, although they can be expensive, and it's best to make sure what the terms of hire are before ordering. If they must be worn, it's advisable that the actor wears his as often as is possible before first night, so that he becomes used to it.

Note that any military or police uniform which you need should only be worn as part of the play and never outside, for their use is carefully controlled by law.

DURING PERFORMANCE

...and if costumes are used in rehearsal, you should

- Name each character's costume before hanging it on the rail. It's a good idea to put small items and trimmings (gloves, jewellery, fans etc) in a plastic bag, labelled and hung over the dress hanger with its appropriate costume.
- Ensure that actors take care of their costumes. You should ask them to cover their costume when applying makeup or drinking coffee during the interval. A stain could ruin all your work. Make sure, too, that they hang costumes back on the rails after use. Check for any

repairs, cleaning or ironing which may be necessary before the next performance, and if you don't have time to do it, ask an ASM or the actor himself to do it for you.

- You and an assistant should be on hand to help the actors to dress, especially if any quick changes are involved. If this is the case, and an actor won't have time to return to the dressing room, you should make sure that any costume needed is hung on a rail in a corner of the wings. If it's a metal rail, it should be bound with fabric so that the hangers don't clatter as they're moved. If any costume changes are to take place backstage, arrange for a full-length mirror to be set against a wall in a corner where it won't be knocked over. There should, of course, be one in a similar position in the dressing room as well. Actors will probably bring their own hand mirrors.

Return all costume promptly, and in good order at the end of a production. If they belong to the group, they should be cleaned, if necessary, before storage. It's a good idea to list which costumes are in any given storage box or cupboard, so that when the next production is planned, you'll know exactly what you have and where it's stored.

LIGHTING TECHNICIAN

It's highly likely that as an amateur group you wouldn't need to appoint someone to act as a lighting technician. You could be playing in a hall where there are no special lighting facilities to help you create various effects, but in that case, your audience wouldn't expect it anyway. You may possibly have one overhead stage light and perhaps two spotlights fixed above the audience and together they'll light the stage perfectly adequately. The spots are the most useful because you should be able to angle them to improve the 'flat' lighting of the stage light, or to highlight one or two specific acting areas. If the lights have dimming switches, so that they can be faded or brought up gradually, so much the better. But if the lighting has a simple two way system, with one switch beside the main hall door, do make sure that that switch is taped over during the show, or you may find someone front-of-house inadvertently plunges the stage into darkness – personal experience shows that it can happen!

However, for a group which does have access to more professional lighting facilities, the following will give you a general idea of what may be used.

Three basic types of lantern are used to light a stage – flood, beamlight and spot.

- **Flood lights** diffuse a wide soft edged beam of light over a large area. They may be set above the proscenium arch at the front of the stage and half way back if the stage is deep enough.
- **Beam lights** in general give a narrower and more intense shaft of light.
- **Spot lights** have a lens which gives a higher concentration of light to a smaller area. Anyone who has seen pantomime will know of the larger more powerful follow spots, which are manually operated so that the beam highlights someone as they move across the stage.
- A **fresnel lantern** (pronounced *fra*-nell) also projects a soft edged beam of spot light, but since the lantern has four 'doors' attached to the front (known as **barn doors**), the size of the beam can be adjusted as well as its direction.
- A **profile lantern** also emits a clearly defined spot, but it's more focusable since it has one or more lens. This lantern may also sometimes be used to create patterns within the beam of light by inserting a 'gobo' between the gate of the lantern and the lens.
- The **gobo** is a thin piece of metal on which a design has been cut out – leaves, for example – which, when directed towards the stage, will project the leaf shapes on to the required area, most effective when a green gel has been inserted into the lantern as well.
- **Gels** are coloured filters placed in front of a lantern's beam of light, which they may soften or add to so creating an effect. Pale gold, pinks or a straw colour give warmth to the light, while a blue filter will produce the cold look of moonlight
- **Strobe lights** have the effect of making an ordinary action appear to be in slow motion. This requires the light to flicker at a speed which can bring on an epileptic fit to anyone susceptible to them. So, if your group ever uses strobe lights, you must warn of their use by placing a clear notice to this effect by the entrance to the venue.

With specially designed lighting, different acting areas of the stage can be lit to different levels, and when dimmers are used the effects are even better, for the light may be gradually increased, or decreased to give the impression of dusk descending perhaps, with colour filters creating a feeling of cold or of warmth.

Lights coming from an **angle** will take away the 'flat' look, which lights placed in a straight line tend to create. So small spotlights placed at angles to the stage (from the wings perhaps), will create a more interesting pattern of light.

Wherever there are changes to a lighting state, these should be marked in the script as LX cues, separately numbered in the same way as are those used for sound effects (see p63).

It is most important that great care is taken when rigging (erecting) any light systems. Whoever is responsible should never work alone, especially if ladders will be used. The electrician should also make sure that any trailing wires, on stage or off, are taped down as soon as possible, so that no-one can trip over them. All equipment must be kept safe at all times. Remember, too, that any form of lighting generates heat, so take care if you have to move lanterns which have just been used, or even have to change a light bulb which has blown. It's easy to forget if you're in a hurry.

Buying and hiring equipment

It's possible to buy or hire stage lighting if you want to, and there will be a supplier listed in your area in the Yellow Pages. There are also web sites which would provide information as well as equipment if any group could afford to buy a lighting rig of some kind.

Note: whether you hire or buy, you must first make sure that the power system in your venue is strong enough to meet the extra demands that a new rig would make on it. It's important to remember too, that anyone who has the chance to use more professional lighting must seek advice first from an electrician with the special knowledge of theatrical lighting.

Sound Technician

Having read the play, the person responsible for sound will work very closely with the director, to whom he is directly responsible before the show (and to the SM/DSM during performance). The director will generally have some ideas about the music and effects he wants to use, but having a knowledgeable sound engineer in the group can be a great help. If you are responsible for 'sound', you may be asked to provide

- **Pre-show music**, played as the audience comes in (and this is generally begun about twenty minutes before curtain up) interval music, and music played once the final curtain has come down on a performance and the audience prepares to leave. In each case the music will need to be chosen with reference to the director and the era or mood of the play, and it may be purely orchestral or with fitting vocals.

- **Music as part of the play**, such as that heard when a radio, gramophone or CD is played as, for example, during the second scene in Act one, of 'Blithe Spirit' when Madame Arcati plays the recording of 'Always'– and we hear it again at the end of the play.

- **Incidental music**, which may be used to link scenes or cover a scene change. This can also be used to suggest or underline a mood before, during or at any given point in a scene. Finding the right music here is quite a specialist job and you could find it time-consuming, but if a director suggests it, he'll generally know what he wants. The skill will then lie in fading it in and out at the right level and at a precise moment, and you do need good equipment for that – which many small amateur groups don't have anyway. But if you doubt just how effective music can be, turn back the sound during a TV drama on a scene where, for example, someone is walking away down a country lane, or entering a room. Without sound, they're doing just that. Good background music, however, will suggest whether the situation will have a happy outcome, or whether evil is lurking in the background somewhere. A TV programme like 'Dr Who' relies quite heavily on incidental music. It moves from adding to the excitement to softening the mood in the quieter moments between the Dr and his companion.

- **Sound effects**, too, may be used to establish the setting of a scene – the obvious example is bird song, which suggests a garden or the countryside, or an owl hooting to suggest night-time. Effects are especially useful in denoting an off-stage event – the arrival or departure of a car, for example, or a marching band, the passage of time (clock chimes), a creaking door, the scream or a gunshot in an off stage murder. Most libraries hold copies of CDs, some prepared by the BBC, which you will be able to borrow.

Effects are also used to heighten an atmosphere, especially when the sound (drumming, for example) grows in intensity and perhaps cuts off suddenly. Both sound effects and atmospheric music should be chosen and used with care, both with regard to the initial choice and to the timing, volume and fading out of the effect. If you cut off a sound suddenly when it would be more effective if faded down slowly, you may ruin the effect which you and the director went to such trouble to establish in the first place.

Before you begin to look for the music/effects, you, as the technician, should, of course, study the play and then attend one or two rehearsals to see how and where they'll be used, and note this in your script.

Once you've found what you need, you should prepare it ready for the show. To do this, you'll have to record from or actually use the sound from a tape, CD or a computer (depending on the equipment available). During rehearsal, you should time what will be needed and then re-record it on to a CD or a computer, in the correct order and ready for use on cue. If you have the facility to fade in and out, it is wise to record a few seconds more than you think you'll need, so as to make sure that you're not left with silence when there should be sound.

You should, if at all possible, return so that it can be played during the latter stages of rehearsal. This will ensure that you're familiar with the script, that you've got the timing right, the director is happy with what you've done and the actors know what to expect.

So, during the technical rehearsal, all that should be necessary, apart from setting up the equipment you're going to use, will be the setting of sound volume to the required level.

Each sound effect, whether it is literally that or a piece of music, should be given a cue number. This makes it easier for you, the director (and the DSM if you're in a theatre) to cue it in at the correct point in the play. So, rather than someone saying 'it comes after John's first speech' the effect can be referred to as FX cue 4, 5 or whatever it may be in the list of sound cues. These cue numbers should be noted in the script where they're to be used, so that you, the technician, know at a glance exactly where they occur, and in the event of your being absent, another member could take over.

In many amateur situations, whoever is responsible for 'sound' will not be given verbal cues but will watch and listen to the play, following the script himself and through familiarity and rehearsal, will know just when to 'press the button'. If you're working in a theatre, the DSM will give the cue over the intercom, but in that case, the DSM will have warned you that it's coming approximately ten lines before it's needed.

Always do a **sound check** each night before the audience enters the venue, to ensure that the system is working correctly. And after each performance, leave the sound script in a safe place so that if you're unexpectedly unable to attend, someone else will find the cued copy ready for use.

Sound Equipment

A new amateur group may have to use home equipment, but this is greatly enhanced if speakers can be fixed near the stage. If you're taking your own equipment to another venue, check that the plugs are compatible and find out whether you'll need to provide extension leads. If you're working in a venue which already has a sound system in place, you should seek advice from whoever's in charge there before attempting to use it.

At no time should liquid or food ever be taken near equipment. After the show, the tapes, discs or computer or whatever you have used, should be packed away, in good order, or the machine just left unplugged if it's really safe to do so.

If you decide to purchase your own sound equipment, you'll find that there are many good mobile systems on the market. These are the kind of machines used by disc jockeys and they have the advantage of having their own amplifiers, and most pack neatly into a travelling case. The Yellow Pages directory or web sites will list any suppliers of sound systems in your area, and if funds allow, this piece of equipment will help to make your amateur drama not only more interesting and effective, but also appear more professional. Since you can use it with a microphone, it will also be useful for public events other than drama. If you do buy your own equipment, it's advised that at least two members of the group learn to use it, so that there's always someone who can become technician for any performance or on any occasion. When not in use, it should be locked away in a safe and secure place.

Property Master

The property master/mistress working in conjunction with the director and the production and/or stage manager will help assemble all the properties needed during a performance. This sometimes includes the furniture, but generally the emphasis will be on small moveable objects, such as those which 'dress' the set – ornaments, books, tea service etc – along with hand properties which the actors use. They should always reflect the period of the play and the setting.

Lists, lists, lists

A list of props is generally found at the back of the play script, but discuss this with the director first, for more often than not he'll amend it. By the time the play reaches the stage, you, the 'props person' if you are wise, will have made out lists to remind yourself and the cast what properties are being used in any given scene and by whom. These lists can be used in rehearsal and even pinned in the wings for general information during performance (see opposite). Points to remember are:

List what you have...

Any item borrowed should be noted down as such, with the name of the owner beside it. It's not advisable, however, to borrow anything of great value, for even any insurance cover you may be able to provide, couldn't make up for its breakage or loss. If an item comes from someone outside the company, it's a courtesy to make some acknowledgement in the programme, not necessarily naming the item unless that would be appropriate, but acknowledging help. If you have difficulty locating something, the editor of your local newspaper or radio station can often be a useful contact. Don't leave your search to the last minute, but once found, arrange to collect the item about a week before performance unless it's something which can't be replicated for rehearsal. In each case, be sure that the owner knows the name of the group or the person they've lent it to (give a receipt if they would like one) and return the item as soon after the production as possible.

Every item entrusted to your care should be looked after, and if it's valuable, it should be locked away between performances. After all, you may want to borrow something again and you must prove yourself, and the group, to be trustworthy.

Most items, especially small ones, such as ornaments, can be labelled underneath with a small removable label stating where they've come from.

... and where it should be.

Items needed for a scene change should be placed as near to the set as possible. If, during performance they're to be placed on the right half of the set (stage right) they're best put ready in the wings on that side, if there's room, with the same pertaining to stage left. This doesn't include items which won't be needed until after the interval, when first act props can be removed and replaced by those which will be needed for any scene change in Act Two. All too often space in the wings is at a premium. Remember that storage boxes should be tidied away and never left where people may fall over them.

Setting the Scene

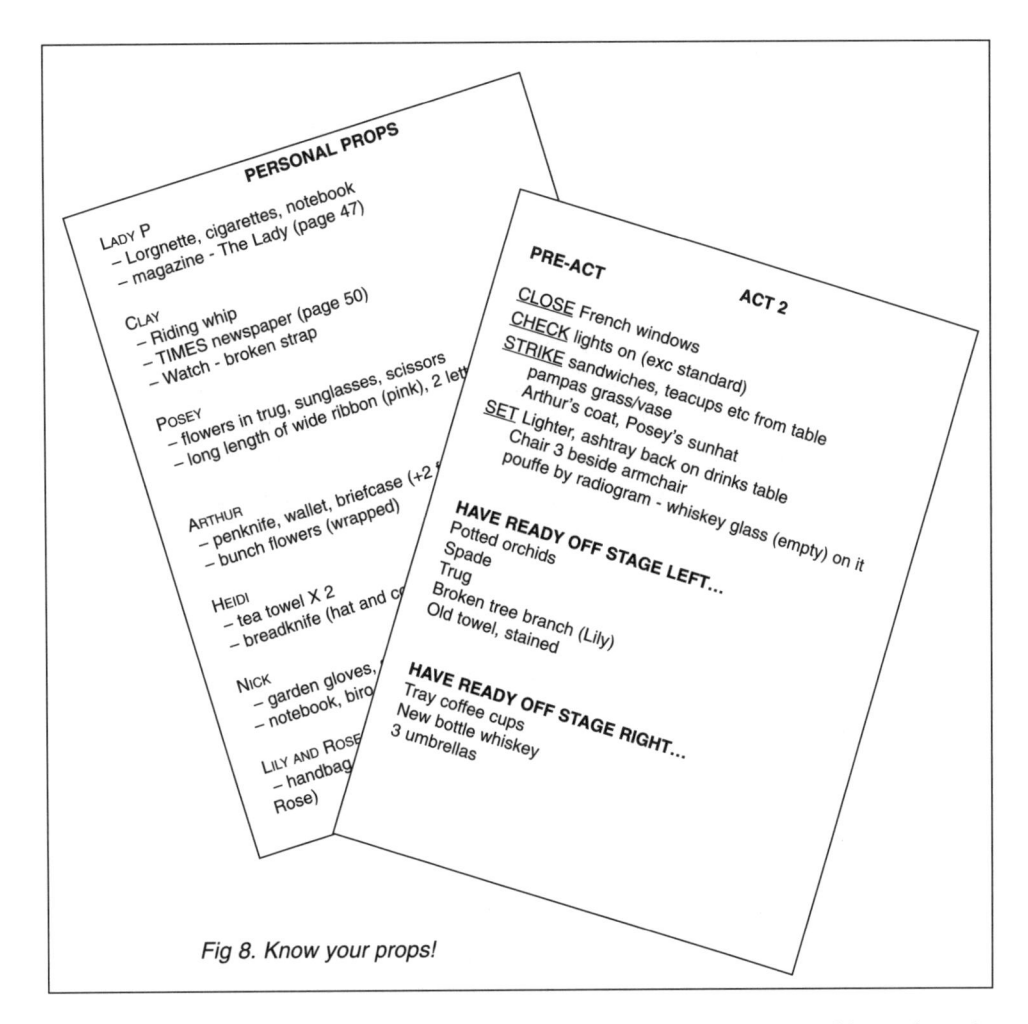

PERSONAL PROPS

LADY P
- Lorgnette, cigarettes, notebook
- magazine - The Lady (page 47)

CLAY
- Riding whip
- TIMES newspaper (page 50)
- Watch - broken strap

POSEY
- flowers in trug, sunglasses, scissors
- long length of wide ribbon (pink), 2 let[...]

ARTHUR
- penknife, wallet, briefcase (+2 [...]
- bunch flowers (wrapped)

HEIDI
- tea towel X 2
- breadknife (hat and c[...]

NICK
- garden gloves,
- notebook, biro

LILY AND ROSE
- handbag
Rose)

PRE-ACT   **ACT 2**

CLOSE French windows
CHECK lights on (exc standard)
STRIKE sandwiches, teacups etc from table
pampas grass/vase
Arthur's coat, Posey's sunhat
SET Lighter, ashtray back on drinks table
Chair 3 beside armchair
pouffe by radiogram - whiskey glass (empty) on it

HAVE READY OFF STAGE LEFT...
Potted orchids
Spade
Trug
Broken tree branch (Lily)
Old towel, stained

HAVE READY OFF STAGE RIGHT...
Tray coffee cups
New bottle whiskey
3 umbrellas

Fig 8. Know your props!

Hand props used by the actors should be placed on a table at the side of the stage from which the actor will enter when he needs it, so that he can pick it up on the way. The table can be sectioned off to provide a space for each actor. This can be done by covering the table with white paper or a sheet, which is then marked into squares by pen or tape, with the character's name in his own square. If a table isn't available or it would take up too much space in the wings, small items can be placed in small boxes or baskets, suitably named, as near to the stage entrances as possible.

You must insist that the actor replaces the item in 'his' section unless he has to leave it on-stage, otherwise you'll spend valuable time hunting down lost properties.

In the event of a big inter-scene change, you and the SM, should organise a team of ASMs who will be responsible for different items, choreographing who removes or sets these if necessary and the order in which the work's done. These changes should become part of the action in the latter stages of rehearsal, so that the change will be done quickly and efficiently during performance.

Props should be available as soon as the actors have dropped their scripts. They don't need to be those which will be used during performance, but they should be reasonable substitutes.

When the show ends on the final night, you'll find that it pays to be really organised for the strike, so make sure that all your lists are to hand. It will help if, during the interval, you can collect any small items not needed for the second half. But make sure that you do this silently in the wings, if you're not setting up for the next act. You might even begin to pack things away if previously hidden boxes can be retrieved, but make sure that the boxes are not in the actors' way and do check the lists to make sure that items are really not needed again.

Special Considerations for Props

Candles/Oil lamps. If candles or lamps are demanded as part of the action, try to use candle bulbs and batteries, or enlist the help of your local fire safety officer, for naked flames are not acceptable on stage. Even if hangings and fabrics have been fireproofed, as indeed they should be, the danger still exists where naked flame is used. An audience would prefer to see an artificial candle rather than to sit worrying in case a draught blows the flame against a curtain, so that they have to leave the hall before seeing the end of the show!

Fires/stoves. If they should look as if they're lit, the effect can be achieved by lighting a red electric light bulb concealed beneath coals or wood.

Telephones should be of the period, with the correct ringing sound controlled off stage by you or the stage manager – but if you don't wish to create an unwanted laugh from the audience, be sure that you can see when the receiver is lifted and the phone answered!

Flowers and plants should be of silk if possible, for real ones will soon droop under the heat of the lights. There's a myth which says that real flowers on stage are unlucky (which, of course they would be if a busy crew forgot to water them each night!)

Letters. If a character has to receive or read one, do make sure that there's writing on the notepaper – preferably the words taken from the script and printed or hand written in the correct form. The actor should know the words anyway, but stick to the script (don't write a silly joke, it could throw the actor), and a blank page would look just that from the front row of a hall. The same applies to an envelope (with the appropriate stamp – make sure it's the right colour), which should be sealed each night. Audiences do notice detail, and attention to detail is the mark of a good property master with professional standards.

China. Don't use precious china, but decorate plain white if it's supposed to be delicate or antique. The same applies to glassware – don't use the best if you can help it. If a tray is used, line it with something which prevents slip (and clatter) – there are such fabrics on the market. It's so easy for an actor or a stage-hand to drop the props if he's nervous or in a hurry. So if possible and as a precaution, set a small dustpan and brush out of sight on set, so that in the event of an accidental breakage a quick-thinking actor could improvise and sweep up the damage before someone is hurt.

Cigarettes. Now that smoking in enclosed public spaces is banned cigarettes may only be used *'where the artistic integrity of a performance makes it appropriate' (The Smoke-free (Exemptions and Vehicles) Regulations 2007)*, as in plays by writers like Noel Coward. The law on smoking during rehearsals is currently being tested, but at the time of writing is considered to be illegal. It may also become law that notices must be posted outside the auditorium in cases where an actor smokes on stage.

If a cigarette must be smoked, (and artificial ones are not very convincing), supply a menthol cigarette and/or a holder if applicable, and make sure that the ashtray used has its base lined with wet sand. If a match is used to light a cigarette, leave a couple sticking out of the box so that a nervous actor doesn't have to struggle to find one. Even if the actor should use a lighter it's wise to have matches on set anyway, for lighters can't always be persuaded to work on cue.

Firearms, along with **knives** and **swords** are subject to stringent safety laws and it's a criminal offence to have a firearm without a police certificate. On stage, it's generally possible to use a gun, if it's been deactivated so that it won't fire live or even blank ammunition, and if it's been checked and stamped by someone with the legal authority to do so. Even then it shouldn't be taken out of the acting area and should certainly not be taken out of the theatre or hall, but locked away when not in use. It's often possible to use, instead, a replica gun or a starting pistol, but if the latter is used make sure that any local regulations are abided by and remember that guns are very noisy and could damage hearing if fired too near someone. In case there's any discharge, which could cause injury, it should be fired with the barrel pointing upwards, at arm's length and to the side of the actor/target – never toward the audience.

In any event, if a weapon must be used and it's not possible to simulate its use by a sound effect, contact your local police who will give advice and issue any necessary certificates.

Drink. Many plays call for wine or whisky (which should never be real!), or tea or coffee and these should be prepared fresh for every performance – although plain water will suffice during rehearsal. You must ensure that in every case both the containers and the glasses or cups are clean and washed after use. Once on-stage for the technical, dress rehearsal and performance, the water should be tinted or diluted to the appropriate colour, and checked for accuracy from the auditorium. Grape juice or a blackcurrant drink makes a good substitute for red wine, grape juice or lemonade for white wine or gin, ginger ale for champagne if sealed in an authentic bottle, and water with food colouring or tea to simulate brandy or whisky. Tea and coffee may be the real thing, but do make sure that it's not too hot!

Food. Again the emphasis is on freshness and hygiene, unless it will be seen but never eaten, when it could be made of plastic, wax or modelling dough. If it has to be eaten, it should be made fresh each night and stored in a refrigerator. Dishes can be 'mocked up' with only a small portion to be consumed set in one area of the plate amid 'dressing', for rarely is there time to eat a whole meal on stage. In many cases bread makes an easy and edible substitute. Brown or white bread soaked in gravy and cut to the necessary shape makes a good substitute for meat. If white, it can become grilled fish when dusted with powdered cornflake crumbs or a fried egg if it has half an apricot set within it. Bananas, too, make excellent alternatives for many foods. Dressings of parsley and lettuce or herbs help to make any dish served in a restaurant scene look authentic. There are many ingenious ways of 'creating' edible food, but whatever you use, test it yourself to make sure that it's pleasant to taste and easily assimilated, and allow the actors to try it out during rehearsal so that they know exactly what to expect. Sometimes the designated food can be used, if it's a sandwich, cake or chips, for example, but often it's possible to substitute the real thing for something less expensive and easier to prepare.

SPECIALISTS

Any amateur drama group may occasionally need to bring in someone with particular skills to help on a production, and in most cases they must be prepared to pay for this expertise, a fact to be remembered when choosing the play. As already noted, this could be an electrician or a carpenter with the equipment and the skill to use it, or someone who will give help with the actors if the director doesn't have the necessary skills. A specialist could also be a

CHOREOGRAPHER

who will design and teach dance, generally for a Musical. Many amateur groups will have someone who could create simple movements for the chorus in a revue, but a full length Musical does require the input of an expert if it's to be successful.

MUSICIAN

Again the group may have a member or a friend who's able to play the piano and this is a valuable talent when it comes to revues and music halls. But if it's a Musical per se, the group will need the services of a musical director and a rehearsal pianist as well as a group of musicians. There are plays, too, which have live music as an integral part of the action, as in a nostalgic country play where someone plays a fiddle or an accordion while the yokels dance. The group must know that they can call upon someone who could help in this way before they decide to stage such a production.

DIALECT COACH

This is sometimes necessary if the group has chosen to produce a play set in a part of the country where there is a strong accent, or if one of the characters happens to speak in a foreign tongue. More often than not, however, there will be someone in the area only too pleased to help the actors speak in an authentic dialect, and this help may cost no more than a ticket to see the play or a small gift. Tape recordings of different dialects are available, and these can be a great help, but they're not really a substitute for someone who can sit by the actor and go through the script with him, while he writes out the words phonetically above those in the text. This is an effective way of learning to speak any required dialect with conviction.

Fight designer

If there's a fight scene in the play, it's sometimes wiser to ask help of someone experienced in choreographing fights or swordplay. These specialists are not always easy to find, although your local theatre may be able to help. If the fight could be described as a minor event, and the director is confident he can work it without injury to the actors, then it should be rehearsed very slowly and carefully, with the participants wearing non-slip footwear. Any weapons should be reproductions of the original, if the authentic item can't be made safe in some way. Safety should be the priority at all times.

9 STAGE MANAGEMENT

what this chapter covers...

You've chosen the play, got the actors and back stage crew, and rehearsals are about to start. What you need now is someone who can co-ordinate the whole process. For most shows, this will be the *stage manager*, ably assisted by a *deputy* and *assistants*. In this chapter we will look in detail at these essential roles.

THE STAGE MANAGEMENT TEAM

THE STAGE MANAGER (SM)

The Stage Manager is the link between the director and the production manager in charge of the physical side of the work needed to stage a performance – although in fact, if it's a small scale production, he may well take on that role as well, and organise a team to help do the work involved. He will also work closely with the director throughout rehearsals and it is his job to see that the public performances run smoothly.

To this end he should, ideally, be a leader of a calm disposition, able to plan ahead, to organise and make decisions quickly, and able to communicate effectively with others. As will be seen, there's much for him to do, and so he should arrange that his assistants (ASMs) help cover the work, so that in many cases he'll take on an over-seeing role, rather than trying to do everything himself. So, if you are Stage Manager, the ability to *organise and delegate* is not only useful, but essential!

GENERAL RESPONSIBILITIES

- You will be responsible for all aspects of the stage area, both in rehearsal and performance, and you must ensure that your assistants know exactly what's expected of them, notifying them of any changes which the director may make, and through regular production meetings, checking that they're happy with what they're doing. Like the props manager, you should be good at making lists!

- You should be aware of all health and safety aspects for every member throughout the production – safety in the hall, stage, wings and dressing areas – and you or the PM should double check to make sure that any wires going across the floor are taped over and any carpets secured so that they don't slip. One member of the crew should never be asked to move a very heavy object, if it really needs two to move it. Should an accident happen at any time during a production, you should record the time, place and manner of the incident in a notebook. You must also ensure, through your property manager, that any food or drink used on-stage is fresh for each performance and that all china, glassware and utensils are washed every time they've been used.
- During both rehearsals and performance you should make sure that any backstage fire exits are unlocked and then locked again before you leave. You must be aware of fire regulations and of exit procedures, and ensure that every member knows what to do in the case of an emergency.
- You should hold a list of the names and telephone numbers of everyone involved in the production. Make sure that everyone has your contact number so that they can inform you if they're going to be late or are unable, for some reason, to attend a rehearsal or a performance. It's often the SM, too, who collects the relevant team information for the programme (cast, crew etc) checking that names are spelt correctly before handing over the list to whoever's in charge of publicity and programme printing. You should also add a list of any acknowledgements for help which are to be included. It's also your responsibility to give a programme to each member of the team on first night, and to collect orders and money for any photographs which the team may order. These jobs, of course, could be delegated to someone else in the group if you're busy.

DURING REHEARSALS
- Unless all rehearsals are held on the stage where the performances will take place, you should mark out the floor space to equate the stage area in performance. If rehearsals take place in a hall used by others, all PVC tape or chalk markings should be removed from the floor after each rehearsal. Often it may be sufficient to mark the edges of the acting area and the doors and windows, by using outward facing chairs.
- In consultation with the director, you should mark any changes that

are made to the text. You must also note in your script how each scene is to be set, and you're responsible, along with members of your team, for seeing that each scene is ready, both during rehearsals and performance. A diagram of the set can be a useful aid to checking that furniture is correctly placed (see p70). Scene changes and set dressing should always be carried out as quietly and efficiently as possible, and to this end, you must make sure that each of your assistants (ASMs) knows exactly what he/she is to do, especially during the final weeks of rehearsal. It helps if you prepare a 'who-does-what' list of scene changes, which can be pinned to a wall in the wings as reference for everyone involved.

- In the beginning you should work beside the director at rehearsal, recording these scene changes in your script, listing all the necessary furniture, set dressing, and sound and lighting cues, if applicable. Make notes to communicate to others if this will be necessary. Your deputy (DSM, see p92) will also be present at rehearsal, noting the actors' moves and also any subsequent changes, along with any extra cues and costume changes, which can be later conveyed to you if you're busy.

- If you have to record lighting and sound cues, you'll find it helpful if you use coloured pens – blue for lighting, red for sound perhaps. In the professional theatre, this work and the responsibility for working with the technicians is taken on by the Deputy Stage Manager, who, during performance, sits at the desk in the prompt corner, cueing lighting and sound as well as giving the actors courtesy calls to ensure that they're ready for their entrances on stage. In an amateur group, you could ask one of your ASMs to act as call-boy so that the actors arrive in the wings a few minutes before they're to go on stage.

GET IN, TECHNICAL AND DRESS REHEARSALS

- You, with the PM, help supervise the get in, making sure, through your team, that everything is ready and in its rightful place. To this end, you should reach the venue at least an hour before the actors arrive, and you must remember to allocate the actors' dressing room space. You must see that the cast leave this tidy after each performance and especially when the show is over.

- If the floor is to be marked so that furniture is set in the correct position for each scene, a small triangle of PVC tape can be placed on the floor behind the upstage corners of each item – and during performance this should be small enough to be left in place throughout the run. Use different coloured tape for each scene setting.

- You should make sure that the audience can't see the actors as they wait in the wings to enter. To do this, check the sight lines from the auditorium during the technical rehearsal, then put down a marking tape at each entrance. Actors must stand behind this if they're not to be seen.

- Traditionally it's you, as SM, who is responsible for running the show after the dress rehearsal, which is why, from the beginning you should appoint and organise your team so that they know exactly what their responsibilities are.

- Before or after the dress rehearsal, it's usual for the SM to address the cast and crew concerning any rules of the venue, and any other rules or regulations which they should observe. These should include what to do in the event of fire, insistence on silence in the wings and a ban on alcohol backstage and in the dressing rooms. Whatever an actor might think, alcohol does affect performance! An adherence to a few rules will help maintain the smooth running of the show and the high standard of production which every amateur company should aspire to.

- You or the DSM should time the Dress Rehearsal, noting also the time of the interval. This information should be given to the Front of House manager at least one hour before performance on the First Night.

- On performance nights, you should arrive before the actors and you're responsible for seeing that they and the crew sign in at 'the half', which is 35 minutes before curtain up, and that they sign out before leaving. You must therefore provide a list of their names in the backstage area for them to sign each evening. No actor should leave the backstage area during performance without your permission. No actor should ever be allowed into the front of house area in costume or make-up unless the play demands it or there is some urgent, exceptional circumstance.

- If an actor will be late or must be absent from any performance, you must contact the director immediately so that contingency plans can be set in place.

- Before the performance, especially if the group is using an outside venue, you must ensure that any actors' valuable items are put away safely until you collect them again for their return after performance.

You must ensure that quiet is observed off-stage at all times and that the crew working backstage wear soft soled shoes and are dressed in black. A visible, noisy crew will ruin the atmosphere, unless, of course, their moves are plotted in as part of the action – and even then they should generally move silently and efficiently.

You, as SM, are responsible for ensuring that interval tea or coffee is available back-stage for the actors and crew during the interval (and during rehearsal). This doesn't necessarily mean you have to make it yourself, but you should organise someone to do it. In an amateur group, it's highly likely that the ladies who provide it each members' evening will be happy to continue to do so during a production – unless they're too busy serving interval drinks to the public.

THE SHOW BEGINS...

On performance nights, having checked that everyone is present and everything's in order, that the stage is ready and the technicians, if there are any, have completed pre-show checks, you should advise the front of house manager that he may open the hall doors. This is generally about thirty minutes before curtain up.

Five minute before the start of the show, when beginners are on stage ready for curtain up and the crew and technicians are in place, advise the front of house manager that you're ready, so that he can check the toilets and clear the foyer. This is when, in a theatre, the DSM uses the loudspeaker system to warn the audience that the show is about to begin. Whether it's in a hall or a theatre, it's the SM who always liaises with the manager. It's usual then, just before the lights go down, for the SM to ask patrons to switch off all mobile phones. Then you should signal for the house lights to be switched off, and the show begins. The sequence is repeated after the interval, see p120.

... AND ENDS

When the curtain comes down after each performance, the SM's main duty is to check that the stage and back-stage areas are tidy and that everything is ready for the next night. To this end, it's wise to set up for the first scene again before you leave, so that it will only be necessary to check everything when you arrive the next night.

STRIKE

There is always a rush to begin the strike. Things can get lost and everything can become disorganised if the necessary lists and packing boxes are not to hand, so be prepared!

Deputy Stage Manager (DSM)

The name says exactly what the role of the DSM is. The DSM heads the list of Assistant Stage Managers, and it is he who often works as the director's liaison officer, passing on any requirements which he may have to the SM or whoever's head of another department – although in amateur drama, since most of the 'heads' will be at rehearsal anyway, the director can generally speak directly to whoever's concerned.

As DSM you are responsible for sitting beside the director during the blocking so that you can note in your script the moves which actors are given. In a small company, you could also become the prompt, for you'll soon be familiar with the script.

Toward the end of the rehearsal period, you should time the scenes, and the full length of the play, and after the Dress Rehearsal, write out a notice giving the times of the interval and end of show. This, you or the stage manager will then pass to the front of house manager.

If the show is being staged in a professional theatre where there's an intercom system to the lighting and sound box, it's the DSM who cues the lighting and sound technicians. In this event, the professional technicians working in the theatre will almost certainly help and advise you.

Assistant Stage Manager (ASM)

Again, the name depicts the role and you, if you're an ASM, will take on the tasks allotted to you by the SM. This will include helping set out the furniture, dress the set, work on any scene changes and do that most thankless of jobs, draw the curtains. In amateur drama you may also be asked to paint and hammer, if you can, and lend a hand with any odd job which needs to be done before (or during) the production.

The Prompt

She, (it's nearly always a woman) is a very necessary part of the team, especially from the actor's point of view! She should attend all rehearsals once the play has been blocked, and will certainly be needed when the cast have put down their scripts.

If you are asked to prompt, you'll find that you almost become part of the cast, for you'll work very closely with them and may even be required to 'read in' if someone is absent. For this reason, it's very difficult for anyone else to take over as prompt once the play reaches the final week of rehearsal and, unless it's absolutely unavoidable, it certainly shouldn't happen once the play's on stage. Being Prompt requires great concentration. Once in regular attendance, you should

- Mark all pauses in the prompt copy of the play, and of course, any cuts.
- Prompt clearly and firmly,
- Make a note of any mistakes or speeches which were paraphrased too much, and then pass this on to the actor concerned when there's a break in rehearsal. It's also a good idea to mark any lines which a particular actor may always find difficult, then you're prepared!

You should make sure that you never allow your attention to wander, for during rehearsal there's nothing worse, when a silence occurs, than to have a prompt say 'Oh, where have you got to?'

Towards the end of the rehearsal period, and if the director's in agreement, it's useful for the prompt to remain silent so that the players are forced to 'get themselves out' of a muddle if things go wrong. This can prove to be a valuable exercise for everyone, if the director can bear the frustration. But at least the actors will be aware of how much they've come to depend on you – and that's something you really don't want them to do during the show.

During performance, you'll sit in the wings, preferably where you can see the actors, but having worked closely with them, you should be able to anticipate where a prompt may be needed and where you know the actor will regain control without your help. It's helpful if you can sit at the same side of the stage during rehearsal, for then the actors will know exactly where your voice will come from, whether it's during rehearsal or performance.

If you do have to prompt during the show, it should be in a firm clear voice, and being almost part of the acting team by then, you'll know whether the first word of the line will be sufficient, or whether you should give a longer phrase or the whole sentence.

Remember to leave the prompt copy in a safe place in the rehearsal room after each meeting and after each performance. This is so that in the event of your not being there on any particular night, someone else can take over and they will have all your notes in the script to help them try to prompt as efficiently as you have done.

10 FROM PAGE TO STAGE

what this chapter covers...

It is the aim of every director to transform the dry stark words printed on the pages of the script into an engaging and memorable performance. There is a lot more to this than just telling the actors where to move.

A good director will know the play intimately, will cast it well, have ideas for set, lighting and sound, and be able to keep morale and enthusiasm up from the first meeting to the arrival of the audience. *And* tell the actors where to move!

In this chapter we look in detail at this most complex of theatre jobs.

THE ROLE OF THE DIRECTOR

Many directors start their lives in amateur drama as actors, and this can be a great help when you come to take on the responsibility of producing a play yourself. Having been part of the process before, you will know what's involved, will find it easier to understand the problems that your actors may face and you should be able to help them perfect their skills. However, it is inadvisable to take part in the play you are directing. Your work will be doubled, and even if yours is only a small role, you won't be able to focus 100% on the other actors because you will have to think about what your character should be doing. It's obvious, too, that if you are actually on stage, you can't get a true and objective overview of what's happening all the time. It's especially unwise to cast yourself, however tempting it may be, if you are working with a relatively inexperienced group, for they are going to need help if their work is to reach a high standard. And in amateur drama you will not only be working with the actors. During rehearsals you will be expected to continue monitoring everything that happens as part of your production.

For some months, from the moment the decision to stage the play has been made and the venue booked, to the end of First Night when the curtain falls – and perhaps, if things go wrong, to the end of the production – you as the Director will live with that play as an integral part of your life. As part of this commitment, you will:

Study the play

Knowing the play well will give you confidence, especially if you are an inexperienced director, as well as an advantage over everyone you will come to work with. They will all study it in time, of course, but your obvious knowledge in the early stages and the ideas you will have about what you want, will give the team confidence in you as well, and they will try their best to do what you ask of them. So before production meetings and casting, you will, if you are wise, begin by reading and re-reading the play to find out as much about it as possible – its theme, the patterns of the plot and the sub-plot(s), where the highs and lows come and what the characters are like. If it's an historical work, like Robert Bolt's 'A Man for All Seasons', for example, it will pay you to do some research into the main protagonists, for they were real people. It will help you to know something about the time in which they lived, the locations and costume, so that you have a more informed picture of what life was like in that era, and in particular, what the characters were like as living people. Whatever the play, by the time you begin to work with your team, you should have some idea of what you are looking for in the actors, the scenic background(s) you wish to set them in, and if you are able to incorporate light and sound, what, if any, special effects you would like to produce. So from just words on a page, the script will change into actions, colour, light and sound as the story takes life on the stage. On the way, it's inevitable that changes will be made, but this will be much easier if you have a vision and a framework in place to begin with.

Prepare your script for use

This can be done as soon as soon as you have your script to work with. The easiest and most effective way of preparing it is to take it apart and interleave each page of script with a plain sheet of paper before setting it in a ring binder. The advantage of interleaving is that if in the early days you make too many mistakes or the moves are all re-blocked, that particular page can be removed and replaced without any interference to the script itself. So facing each page of text is a blank sheet on which you can make notes, draw diagrams of the set and note an actor's moves in relation to the action within that page of script. It goes without saying that all moves, whether they are notes or little diagrams, should always be done in pencil, for inevitably you will make changes as you work, and rubbed out notes are much neater and easier to follow than crossed out biro.

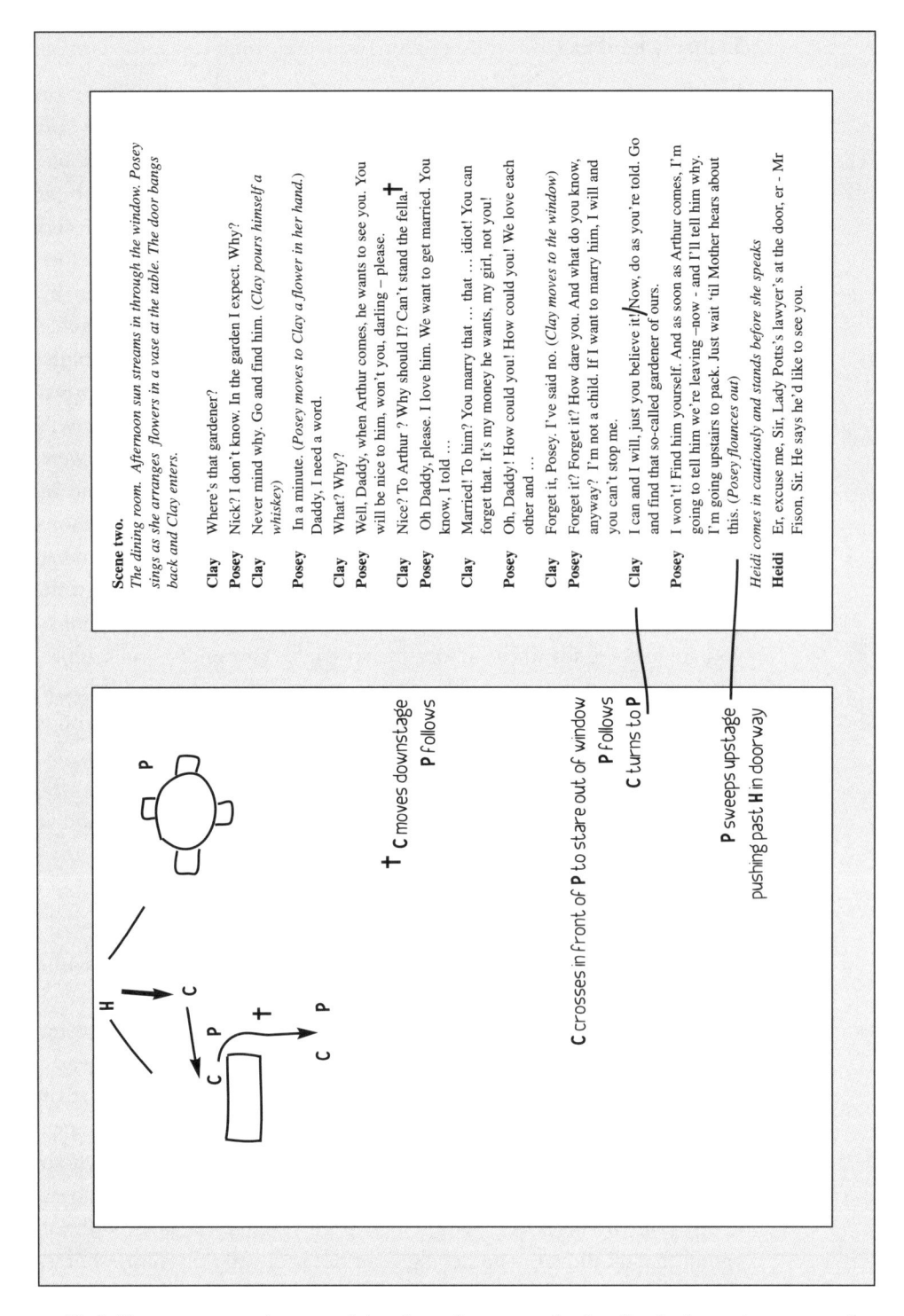

Scene two.
The dining room. Afternoon sun streams in through the window. Posey sings as she arranges flowers in a vase at the table. The door bangs back and Clay enters.

Clay Where's that gardener?
Posey Nick? I don't know. In the garden I expect. Why?
Clay Never mind why. Go and find him. (*Clay pours himself a whiskey*)
Posey In a minute. (*Posey moves to Clay a flower in her hand.*) Daddy, I need a word.
Clay What? Why?
Posey Well, Daddy, when Arthur comes, he wants to see you. You will be nice to him, won't you, darling – please.
Clay Nice? To Arthur ? Why should I? Can't stand the fella.
Posey Oh Daddy, please. I love him. We want to get married. You know, I told …
Clay Married! To him? You marry that … that … idiot! You can forget that. It's my money he wants, my girl, not you!
Posey Oh, Daddy! How could you! How could you! We love each other and …
Clay Forget it, Posey. I've said no. (*Clay moves to the window*)
Posey Forget it? Forget it? How dare you. And what do you know, anyway? I'm not a child. If I want to marry him, I will and you can't stop me.
Clay I can and I will, just you believe it! Now, do as you're told. Go and find that so-called gardener of ours.
Posey I won't! Find him yourself. And as soon as Arthur comes, I'm going to tell him we're leaving –now - and I'll tell him why. I'm going upstairs to pack. Just wait 'til Mother hears about this. (*Posey flounces out*)

Heidi comes in cautiously and stands before she speaks

Heidi Er, excuse me, Sir, Lady Potts's lawyer's at the door, er - Mr Fison, Sir. He says he'd like to see you.

† **C moves downstage**
   P follows

C turns to P

C crosses in front of P to stare out of window
P follows

P sweeps upstage
pushing past H in doorway

Fig 9. Two-page spreads are useful as they allow space for the director to mark moves and make notes directly opposite the pages of the script.

It means, too, that everything connected with the production can be contained within this one ring binder, even to the extent of having A4 plastic sleeves at the back, in which you can tuck receipts, photographs, lists – and there will be many – and any other small odd bits of information which will be collected over the weeks to come. Experience shows that they will surely be lost if they are not methodically tucked away safely in the file.

Map out the framework of the play

Having become familiar with the script, it can help to map it out so that you can see the pattern of scenes for each character and how he/she relates to the others. Most directors have their own way of doing this, whether it's by using a graph or some other method (see Fig. 9, opposite). It can be a very effective way of looking at how the play is made up, where the scenes change, where different characters come together, where there are highs, conflicts and lows in the action. So, having done your 'map', you should be able to divide the play into sections ready for rehearsal.

A diagram like this can also be useful during the auditioning process if/when you want to hear actors' voices, one against the other, or wish to compare them physically. It is invaluable, too, when you come to work out the rehearsal schedule which you may be required to fit round actors' holidays or other unavoidable absences. In both cases, the plan shows at a glance when different characters work together on a scene, and this makes it easier for the director who can see, without having to flick through the script, on which pages this happens.

Consider the design of the set – exits, entrances & windows

Your study will suggest any changes you may have or wish to make to the original set design. It is possible that exits and entrances used in the script can't be reproduced on your stage. Many halls have no doors leading directly off a stage, only curtains. In that case, they will have to be pulled aside or looped up and if there is no way of setting a door within flats, both actors and audience must imagine that wooden door banging as a character storms off – something everyone seems to accept without any trouble, just so long as the actor believes there really is a door there! So, knowing the circumstances within which you must work, you will set doors and windows where they will best serve the action of your play. Unless it is physically impossible, you should have at least one entrance on stage left, another on stage right, and preferably

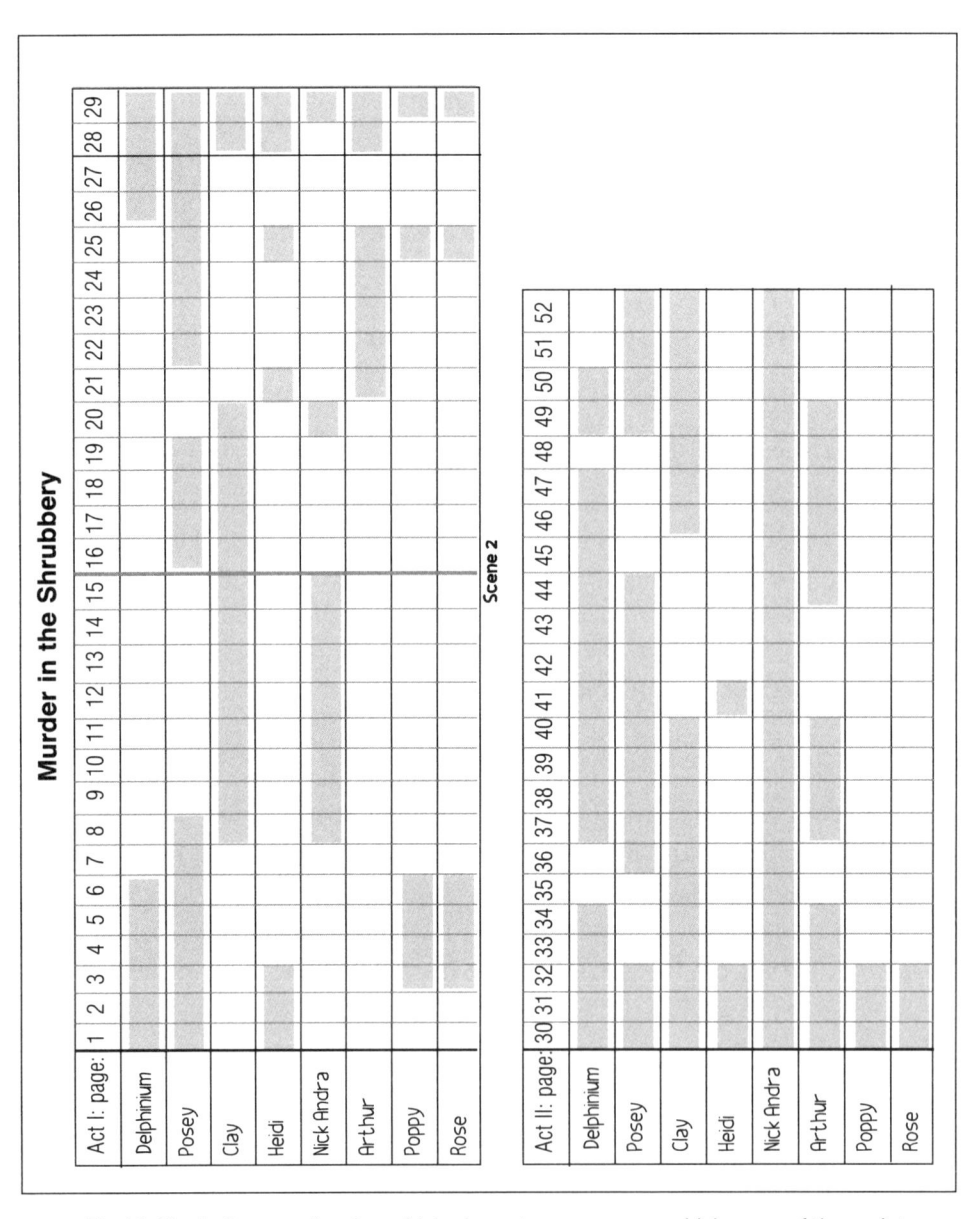

Fig 10. Block diagram showing which characters appear on which page of the script

one upstage. An entrance upstage centre is very useful, for characters can make commanding entrances and exits from that position, and it makes for more interesting movement.

Incidentally, it's most unlikely that there'll already be a window where the action of the play demands it and a suggestion as to how this may resolved can be found on p70.

LIST DESIRED FURNITURE AND FURNISHINGS

You must also decide what furniture you will need, and on a small stage this is best kept to essentials. Actors can't move freely round a cluttered stage and as a general rule, the less furniture there is, the larger the space will appear. It has already been noted (on p63) why heavy high-backed furniture should be avoided.

Furnishings, too, are important in setting a scene and they, as well as the furniture itself, should reflect both the era and the social standing of the characters. If at all possible, the colouring of the furnishing should be chosen in conjunction with the costume design (see p77). If you, as director, can decide as early as possible just what your requirements are, it will give the Production Manager or Stage Manager and his team more time to find or prepare what's needed, or to change something if it's found to be unsuitable. Any director who decides on dress rehearsal night that he doesn't, after all, like the colour of the set will have a mutiny on his hands!

THINK ABOUT THE SOUND AND LIGHTING EFFECTS

These should be an integral part in setting both mood and scene, and as you study the play you should come to know what you'd like these effects to be — although for many amateur groups the facilities are not available. Even the music your audiences hear as they enter the hall should echo the tone of the play, and this is something all companies should be able to organise. You may already know what music you want and you will almost certainly know what effects you'd like to create through lighting — that is if you have lighting which is capable of being more than 'stage light on/off'.

As soon as possible you should discuss your ideas with the rest of the production team at the meeting you will have with them before the play is cast. This gives you and the technicians plenty of time to look for music and to design a lighting plan, if applicable. Further information on effects is given on p77.

CALL A PRODUCTION MEETING

As soon as you think you know what you hope for and decisions have been made as to who will be working backstage, you should meet with the members who will be directly involved to discuss how best your ideas can be achieved. In an established company this can and should be done at a production meeting before auditions are held, so that definite plans can be made and the potential cast given some idea of what they will be working on. More often than not in an amateur group, especially a new one, it's not possible to delegate production or backstage responsibilities until the actors have been cast. If this is the case, a production meeting for the crew should be held before rehearsals begin, so that everyone involved knows what lies ahead. They should also be held occasionally during the rehearsal period as a check that everything is going to plan, with a final one just before the Get In.

CASTING THE PLAY

It often happens when a director is reading a play that he will begin to have ideas as to who among the membership could play certain characters. Some of this knowledge will come from having seen members in previous acting roles or watched them participate in workshop activities, and this could be another reason for using the exercises in Section 3 as part of group meetings. You may even instinctively hear the voice of a member saying certain lines. It is, however, most important that no decisions are made before an audition. You could check that the member in mind will be attending audition, (and give no promises) but every member who wishes to read a part should be given the opportunity to do so. Sometimes it can be someone quite unexpected who, in the end, turns out to be the right person for a particular role.

THE AUDITION

Before any audition, you should mark the passages you will use when asking people to read, whether as a group or individually; passages which bring out character and highlight events. This means that during the audition you won't have to read the whole play from beginning to end, which is something anyone interested should have already done. As it is, if several people want to read for the same part you may well have to repeat your chosen sections: in all fairness, they should be heard reading the same speeches.

Notice of the audition should be circulated among members, possibly by the secretary. If the group wishes to attract new members a notice could also be placed on a notice board or in the local paper, although in that case notification should only state the play's title and author along with the audition time, venue and a contact number. However

DANEMERE AMATEUR DRAMA GROUP
AUDITION NOTICE
'MURDER IN THE SHRUBBERY' by ALAN PORTER.

Director   Belinda Brown

Production   Wed. 21st – Sat. 24th November 2007, Danemere Village Hall.

Audition   Mon. 3rd September at 7.30 in Danemere Village Hall.

Scripts may be borrowed throughout August from Joan West, but please return all copies by the end of that month. Rehearsals will be on every Monday and Thursday from mid September.

The cast:

Lady Delphinium Potts – mid 40s, tall, angular, refined, unpopular. We see her even when she's dead, for invisible to the others, she moves among the players, comments on them and addresses the audience.

Sir Clay Potts, her husband – 50s, rich, well-built, florid, short-tempered fish dealer.

Posey Potts, their daughter – 20s, pretty, spoilt, doted on by her parents.

Arthur Fison – 35, handsome, ambitious, Posey's fiancé and Lady P's lawyer.

Nick Andra – 70s, family gardener, thin, dark-browed, appears sub-servient.

Heidi Ann – 20, the maid, a thin, pale-faced mouse of a girl.

Neighbours – Poppy and Rose, any age, have a few lines each.

The Play, a comedy of blood, fish and bone among the roses, is in two acts. Everyone has gathered for the official opening of the new rose garden, but when the body of Lady Potts is found in a shallow grave beneath the lilac, the household of Sir Clay is thrown into uproar. There are plenty of suspects. The only trouble is, they all admit responsibility. Over the course of one summer evening Nick Andra, the old gardener and amateur sleuth, must unravel the mystery before the police arrive in the morning. What start out as simple false alibis for each member of the family rapidly descend into ever more outrageous claims of guilt, as each one wants the glory of having rid the world of Lady P. I'm sure we'll have some fun with this!

Crew. Anyone wishing to join the team by working on the production in any way will be very welcome on audition night. Do come along and hear what it's all about. The actors can't do the play without help from those who put the production together or work backstage, so come and join the fun. Anyone who wishes to be part of this production but is unable to come on 3rd Sept. is asked to contact me as soon as possible. Thanks. Look forward to seeing you,

Belinda

Fig 11. Example of an audition notice.

you advertise it the notice should appear at least three weeks before the audition date so that anyone interested has time to read the play.

The notice for members should state time and place of both audition and performance, and – if you know them – the evenings on which rehearsals will be held. You should list the characters, their ages, physical appearance and relationship to other characters, if applicable, along with details of any speeches you want to hear. It is usual to say briefly what the play's about. This is a good opportunity to add, too, that anyone interested in working in any capacity other than acting would be very welcome to come to the audition so that they can see what the play is about. One person volunteering to take on a backstage job is worth two who are press-ganged into it!

Scripts should be available on loan for a limited time, but all should be returned before the date of the audition. A notebook kept with the scripts will enable members to record both when they borrow a copy and the date it's returned.

Most groups like to have a committee member, or the membership secretary, sitting in on audition so that there can be no question that it has been run fairly. You may also welcome having someone beside you (preferably someone who knows what directing a play is about) who can listen to your ideas and maybe give opinion on the readings, both of which help in the decision making process.

There are several ways of holding an audition, but in every case members should have been given the opportunity to read the play for themselves first, even if the group has read it together. Some find sight-reading difficult and may not be able to show, without having practised, how convincing they could be in character.

Running an audition

The audition will progress smoothly if, on arrival, all members are asked to sign in: name and phone number, with the part(s) they wish to audition for, along with any dates when they know they would not be available for rehearsal. The secretary or another group member could help with this. If there's a space there too, for any non-actor who has come along because they are 'just interested', you will have the names of possible willing back-stage workers to hand. You might also suggest at this point that any actor not cast could consider joining them as a member of that other, most important, team for this production.

The list will help you in two ways: you will have in front of you the names of those wishing to read for each part; and you will know when you wouldn't see someone at rehearsal. Both are vital when considering who to cast, and when drawing up the rehearsal schedule. No actor should be given a part if he is unable to attend most of the rehearsals when his character is part of the action. Missing the odd night through illness or an unavoidable event is acceptable, but absence makes it difficult for other actors involved in that particular scene. From the beginning, actors should understand that they must be prepared to commit fully to any role which they accept, especially if it's a major one.

Having briefly explained how you see the production, the audition itself can begin. Auditions may be held on a one-to-one basis, with each member coming in alone to read for the part, but this can be intimidating. Better for all, especially new, inexperienced members, if the audition takes the form of an informal read-around of parts of the play which include the sections you've chosen, with those wanting to read certain characters taking those parts in turn. A read-around has the advantage of allowing you to hear how voices contrast or blend and how actors would 'match' each other in height and physical characteristics. You have the opportunity, too, of asking members to read a specific part, even though they themselves may not have thought of doing so.

It is also helpful if, once most of the readings have been heard, actors are asked to move about in character as part of the audition, for it will give some indication as to whether they can move well. Some actors can give an excellent reading but once on stage find it difficult to move without appearing wooden – although if you've already seen members working on improvisations during meetings, you will have some idea of how good they can be playing in character.

The audition process should continue until everyone is satisfied that they have read for the character they wish to play, even those who, in your mind, would not be suitable. Any actor should also have the opportunity of talking to you, or reading privately at the end of the audition if he wishes to. Anyone failing to be cast in the part he wanted will at least feel that he had the opportunity of showing his talent and, having heard everyone else as well, will probably recognise when the play's in rehearsal that you cast the right person in the role after all.

It is always best not to announce your casting decisions at the audition, but give a date by which actors will be told if they have been given a part. It is a courtesy to let everyone know by that date whether they have been successful or not. This will give you time to reflect on what you have heard and to call back actors if you can't decide between two or three of them, so making sure that you have cast the most suitable actor in the role.

TYPE CASTING

It is possible that this could be the safest route for any new director, for he'll be casting someone who obviously already has some of the qualities the role demands and the actor involved would probably feel happier playing a character he can readily recognise. Then, too, physical characteristics could influence your choice. An actor with a naturally shrill voice in unlikely to be convincing as a sultry Latin lover, and a heavy-footed actor would find it difficult to play a will'o'the wisp. But casting to type should not be the general rule, for every actor welcomes the chance to take on a role which would be a challenge. Within reason, once they have had some experience on stage, your actors should be given the opportunity to try playing the type of character they have never played before. It is possible that the shy boy would make a very convincing gangster, while the naturally bubbly blonde who is generally cast as the femme fatale, might become a very convincing high powered boss or anguished mother.

BLOCKING

Blocking is deciding on, and marking, the moves actors will make on stage. Before rehearsals begin, block the first scenes, if not the whole play.

Most plays have stage directions printed in italics so that the actor knows when he should move and where he should be at any given time, and these are generally moves which either the author or the play's first director decided should be used in production. Some directors, especially if they have not had a great deal of experience, follow these moves to the letter, without realising, perhaps, that considering the circumstances in which they are working and the space they have to use, it might be more effective if the some of them were changed.

An experienced director will, as he reads a play, see in his mind where the characters are and the moves they make, and although they may not be the same as those printed, they will generally be more effective, given the space in which they will be made in this particular production. You as director can check your moves as you plan your work at home by moving small cardboard figures round a mock-up of the floor plan, matching the moves you envisage to the text. This will show you if one move counteracts another, or if one actor might mask someone else. As you work, pencil in a diagram on the blank page opposite the text (see Fig 9 on p96). You could even head some of the pages with a small diagram showing where the characters are at that time. This can be particularly useful if you have to begin a rehearsal in the middle of a scene.

This preparation can be a time-consuming business, but it can be done in the privacy of your own home at times to suit, and it does save time in rehearsal. It can also save you the embarrassment of always having to move your actors around like pawns, in a way which clearly shows you are not sure what you want. Actors lose confidence in a director who dithers. But it's only in rehearsal, when the actors try them out, that you will really know whether your ideas work If they don't, be prepared to make adjustments. In any event, you should always be one step ahead of the cast, and block the moves for each scene before you meet them in rehearsal.

To move or not to move ...

You may or may not follow the stage directions printed in the script. That's up to you, but remember, actors should *always* have a *reason* for moving, whether it's to move away or towards someone or something, (or to pour a drink, perhaps, which often seems to happen.) Movement can be made as an expression of emotion (anxiety, ecstasy), or as an integral part of the character. Dialogue and characterisation will point where these moves could or should be.

It is your responsibility to plot this changing pattern of moves so that they never look contrived, but appear perfectly natural. You may find in rehearsal that the moves you have plotted don't work as well as you had imagined, or that an actor feels unhappy with his move for a very valid reason. In fact, if you ever have to read in because someone is absent, you will get a whole new perspective on a scene: you will certainly discover whether what you have plotted feels 'right'. Experienced actors often have an instinct for movement and where you have one who has a long speech, you can give him the opportunity of moving at will, with the proviso that he's at point x in your plan by the time he concludes the speech. Rehearsals are there, after all, so that you can correct any mistakes, change any moves. At least if you plan first you will have something to use as a starting point.

GROUPING

How you group the characters is important. There is nothing worse than seeing actors standing in a straight line like birds on a wire, or in a perfect semi-circle. A group should look interesting and pleasing to the eye. It's your job to create suitable 'pictures', which will underline an emotion or mood and enhance your play, although your audience might only recognise and appreciate this fact subconsciously.

The dominant figure in a scene generally takes an upstage, commanding position and the fact that many stages are raked slightly higher at the back can make this easier. The use of steps or stairs can also give dominance to a character, as indeed does one character standing above another who's sitting. Even different heights of furniture can help when forming a group – it is just another part of plotting which should be borne in mind. (Furniture can also be used to great effect in comedy, as seen in Alan Ayckbourn's play 'Table Manners' when Norman is forced to sit at the dining table in a much lower chair than the other diners.)

Avoid moves which force actors to make a 'scissor' movement. This happens when two actors cross while moving in opposite directions at the same time.

Sometimes an actor will appear more in character if he moves very little, but spends much of his time sitting. In fact, some lines are definitely lines when an actor may instinctively feel he ought to sit or stand when saying them, even though you may not think this to be the case at this stage. The more experienced an actor, the more instinct he will have with regard to body language and movement, so in rehearsal always be prepared to work with his instinct, or at least let him try out whatever feels 'right' to him.

To avoid arguments later, insist that actors always pencil in the moves as they are blocked or changed, and give them time to do so.

PACE

When you are studying the text, you will become aware of the pace at which any given scene should be played. Every play has a climax, but there will also be other minor 'highs' and 'lows' within some scenes. You should mark these in your script even at this early stage, so that at a later point in rehearsal, perhaps when the books are down, you can check whether the actors are naturally highlighting these themselves. You may have to point out where you believe changes of timing or mood occur and if necessary orchestrate the emotions or actions of the characters so that the play is given added pace and interest. This ensures that your play in performance will never become monotonous, as any story does if read aloud on one even note.

THE REHEARSAL SCHEDULE

Once you have the dates when you know that you have a working space for rehearsal, when you've cast your actors and know when they would or wouldn't be available, you can set down a rehearsal timetable. If you are careful to work round an actor's previously stated commitments, you will have every right to expect him not to miss a scheduled rehearsal unless something totally unavoidable happens. A pre-planned schedule ensures that everyone knows, from the beginning, the commitment required and they will be less likely to accept a sudden invitation to go elsewhere at that time. It should be understood, however, that the schedule will not include those evenings when two or three actors who share a scene or some dialogue may be expected to get together somewhere to rehearse by themselves. This, and home study away from the rehearsal room, is essential if lines are to be learned by the 'books down' date.

The time required to bring the play up to performance standard will naturally depend on the play itself, how often you have space to work in, your previous experience as a director and on how experienced your actors are. Ideally the cast should work together two or three times a week, but this isn't always possible since, being an amateur group, members must fit drama meetings round other commitments in their lives. A long rehearsal period may be necessary for a complicated play or a first pantomime, but as a general rule, working on a production for more than three months will see boredom set in and enthusiasm wane. More experienced amateur groups, who are fortunate in having frequent access to rehearsal space and *are* able to meet three times a week, can produce a full length play in six weeks or eight at the most. But the longer the gap between rehearsals, the more difficult it is to consolidate performance, or learn the lines. Lines are always more easily remembered through frequent repetition during rehearsal.

Murder in the Shrubbery. Rehearsal Schedule.

The pages noted are those I hope to do. As usual you'll need to work away from rehearsal whenever possible. Note extra rehearsal Fri. 16th. Brackets round your name denote when you're away and someone will read in.
Rehearsals start at 7.30 prompt.

Mon. 3rd Sept.	Read through	
Thurs. 6th	Block 1 – 19	(Nick 8pm)
Mon.10th	Work 1 – 19	(Nick 8pm)
Thurs. 13th	Block 20 – 29	
Mon. 20th	Work 20 – 29	
Thurs. 27th	Act one	

(Fri 28th Production meeting)

Mon. 1st Oct.	Block 30 – 40	
Thurs. 4th	Block 41 – 52	
Mon. 8th	Work 30 – 40	
Thurs. 11th	Work 41 – 52	
Mon. 15th	Act two	
Thurs 18th	As necessary	(Delph)
Mon. 22nd	Act one	(Arthur)
Thurs. 25th	As necessary	
Mon. 29th	Work 30 + as far as possible	

(Tues. 30th Production Meeting)

Thurs. 1st Nov.	Act two
Mon. 5th Nov.	Acts one and two
Thurs. 8th	As necessary
Mon 12th	Run the play (+ costume)
Thurs 15th	As necessary
Fri. 16th	Run play
Mon 19th	Technical rehearsal
Tues. 20th	Dress rehearsal
Wed. 21st	First Night!
Sat. 24th	Last night and strike

Thanks!. *Belinda*

Fig 12. Sample rehearsal schedule.

GENERAL RULES OF REHEARSALS

Timing

- When planning the rehearsal schedule, make sure that you give yourself more time than you think you will really need, because more often than not, you will need it after all! It is better to be able to tell actors that because everything is going so well, they can have an unexpected evening off than to have to demand more rehearsal time because you have underestimated how long it would take to get it right. The wise director will always plot into the second half of the schedule evenings designated for scenes (or sections of them), which may require extra work during the final weeks – otherwise known as the 'polishing' stage of a production. These evenings can be specified by blanking that date with a phrase such as 'if necessary' and actors must understand that they may be called for that rehearsal if they are involved in the extra work that's needed.

- Begin each rehearsal promptly at the stated time, and end it at a reasonable hour. Many amateur actors will have been at work during the day, and will be the following day, and the later the hour you rehearse the less likely they are to remember what they are supposed to do. There's always a great deal to get through during a rehearsal, time has a habit of flashing by and no-one will want to stay late to finish a section because you began twenty minutes late. If a character is late, someone else should read in the lines until he arrives and the latecomer should try to be on time in future, for his not being there when needed affects those he is working with. If an actor knows that he will be late or absent for some unavoidable reason, he should let you or the stage manager know so that you could perhaps work on a different section using the actors who are present – your 'framework map' (p98) will tell you at a glance if that would be possible.

- If four or five actors are required for a certain scene but one doesn't actually appear on stage until some time after the others, he could be allowed a late arrival – for rehearsal, not on performance nights – and his expected arrival time should be noted on the rehearsal schedule. If you are thoughtful enough to allow him this leeway, you can rightly expect him to grant you the same courtesy and arrive in good time for his entrance, otherwise that privilege is withdrawn.

Divide the action

Rehearse the play in sections and have in mind before each one what you wish to achieve, whether it is to establish a character's motivation or his relationship with others, to create an atmosphere or mood, or to underline a point in the plot. Encourage the actor to make notes in the script as he goes along to help him to remember what is required. Working in sections means that there's not too much information for anyone to digest at any one time. Rehearsing a play straight through from beginning to end is rather like eating the dishes of an eight-course meal one after the other without a break. The result is indigestion and the diner has difficulty remembering what each dish was. So repeatedly going straight through an act in the early stages is confusing for everyone. It is better to repeat each section two or three times until there's continuity and understanding before moving on to the next one. Gradually sections can be run together until everyone is sure of what they are doing That's when a scene or an act can be run from beginning to end. This 'section at a time' process brings to the actor a familiarity with both words and moves, which stays with him and makes learning lines easier.

Team spirit

Work in partnership. Having studied the play, you will know what you hope to see in the final performance and it is your job to lead the actors toward this, so that gradually the script lifts from the page to the stage. To do this successfully, you must allow the actors to have some input into what they are doing. You shouldn't impose your vision like a dictator – (after all, the word *producer* comes from the Latin verb, 'producere', which means 'to lead forth'). Be prepared to listen to ideas from the actors – preferably after a rehearsal and not in the middle of it when that could break the flow – and allow them to try them out. Only if the ideas clearly don't work should they be discarded. The same rule applies with gestures. They should come from the actor as he becomes the character he is playing, so give him time to find them himself before feeling that you must impose them.

Consideration

Anyone just watching, or actors waiting for a cue and therefore not on the set, must not be allowed to talk. They should show consideration for those who are rehearsing. Peripheral chatter, or even a whispered conversation, can infuriate a working actor who is desperately trying to concentrate. An actor not directly involved in a scene should sit quietly and watch – and one can always learn from watching others – or sit in another room, or in a corner if there isn't one, and learn his lines. Waiting round for any length of time shouldn't happen if the schedule has been carefully worked out, but it is inevitable that there will be occasions when actors are not required for a while.

AUDIBILITY

Initially you should stand near the actors so that you can guide them as to what you want without shouting instructions from a distance. Then, as rehearsals progress, you should sometimes move towards the back of the hall so that you can tell if anyone is not audible. If they are working in a small room, but will be staging the play in a larger venue, it is important that you insist that the actors project their voices from the beginning. It is a complete waste of time for an actor to learn his lines if no-one can hear them in performance!

THE SET

If at all possible, have the design of the set marked out in some way from the very first 'walking' rehearsal, with 'rehearsal' furniture in the position it will be in performance – but not personal props, these will come later when the actor has a free hand with which to hold them. If working in a floor space and not on a stage, the set should be as near as possible in size to that in the performance venue.

THE REHEARSAL PERIOD

THE READ THROUGH

The full team – actors, stage management and the heads of the various departments – now come together to read the play and begin work on the production, and you should make sure that they all know who's who. If they have not already got them, they should receive their copy of the script along with the rehearsal schedule, on both of which they should write their name and phone number. Someone will lose one or the other before the work is done!

Having heard a brief description of your 'vision' of the play, the cast, still sitting, begin to read it through. The actors will then hear who is playing which character and they can begin to discuss what the characters are like and how they interact. This is the time, too, when the layout of the set is explained and it is a great advantage if there is a model of it, however simple, or at least a diagram. There should have been a production meeting prior to this and so you and the production manager, or whoever is in charge of the physical side of building the set, will be there to answer any questions about that, as well as any other queries which anyone may have. Incidentally, it is helpful if you can tell the actors, even now, which way the doors will open so as to avoid confusion during rehearsal. Ask them to make a note of this, and if, later, it has to be changed, do remember to tell them. If they don't know and the set is rather fragile, the consequences could be catastrophic! Unless it is a very short play, the reading, with the exchange of information and a social coffee break, could take the whole evening. Hopefully, as this first meeting closes, everyone will leave feeling confident and looking forward to working together on the production.

As for a coffee break, whether you continue to have one during every rehearsal is up to you. It can serve as a short break from working, when everyone has the chance to relax and get to know each other, and it does foster the team spirit which every production must have if it is to be successful – but you will have to be strict about enforcing the time given or gossip will take over. Alternatively, actors could make a drink when they are not needed on set, but then you will need a runner to warn them when they are needed again. The decision is yours.

The first rehearsal and those which follow see the beginning of the blocking and then a gradual increase of work on the script. Over the weeks that follow you should see

- The action begin to flow. Blocking is best explained a few pages at a time when the moves are pencilled in before the actors walk them through. Once they prove to work they should be repeated to make sure the action flows before moving on to the next section, until gradually basic movements throughout that scene are all in place. This will happen to each scene in turn, until finally the whole play is blocked and being worked in detail, as planned in your original schedule.

- The characters begin to grow. It is during these weeks that actors will begin to know the characters they are playing and bring them to life through speech and body language. There should be discussion on the characters, what makes them tick, their relationships, aspirations, actions and reactions and the physical expressions of their being. If previously used during ordinary meetings, some of the exercises in Section 3 may help solve some of the problems which could arise now, whether in speech or intonation, body language or imagination. If you have time, taking a few minutes to look at them again (whether as specific exercises or for improvisation) may help your actors in their performance.

Occasionally you reach a plateau when a scene just does not play as it should. The it may refresh a jaded team to spend a few minutes improvising. (If Tituba and the girls spent ten minutes improvising the witchcraft scene from act one of Arthur Miller's 'The Crucible', for example, it might help them bring more realism and tension to their recounting of it.) Or try changing the style of playing for a 'difficult' section. Suggest that the actors play as if doing melodrama, using extravagant gestures, or change it to farce, playing faster than usual, or use only mime to accent the mood you are trying to create. After this one rehearsal you should see that difficult section in a new light and that will help everyone play the scene as the writer intended.

This is the time when every actor should study his character and experiment with different ways of portraying him, so be prepared to allow them to do this at first. Eventually, with your help in rehearsal and their own home study of the text, the actors will not only find the truth of the person they are playing, but will also begin to understand the shape and rhythm of the play, its tensions and lighter moments. They will learn the importance of using timing, pace and pauses, which together help make the script natural and the story alive and interesting. But remember that no actor can really find his character, and certainly cannot portray him convincingly, until he knows the words, so make sure that the cast knows that there is a date on the schedule when you will expect that.

- Lines have been learned. The growth and expression of character through dialogue is a gradual process, and this growth generally moves through four stages:
  - at first the words will still be 'on the page', seen through the eyes and read without a great deal of thought or feeling
  - then through practice and familiarity, some expression will gradually come into the voice
  - then, as the lines are studied in more depth so that the feelings they convey are understood, the actor will begin to express himself through various speech patterns and body language – the lines are spoken more from the heart now

– when he fully understands his character and knows the lines so well that it's almost as if he's digested them, the actor will at last act and react emotionally and physically, and with truth. He'll speak with belief and conviction, a conviction which seems to come from every fibre of his body. You, as director, will notice that he's no longer just listening for his cue line, he's listening to everyone and everything on stage, completely immersed in what's happening around him in the world of this play. Now the actor *is* the character and is not simply acting the part. Not every actor will reach this stage before first night, (and some may never achieve it at all) for it's a fine line and it can take a great deal of study and thought. But when you see it you will recognise it, for it makes any character completely believable for the whole time he's on stage and even when he isn't.

These stages take time but try not to rush the process – just be encouraging and helpful and keep a close eye on the progress.

- Scripts down. A date should be marked on the rehearsal schedule as being the last time when scripts may be held. This can be done an act at a time, but actors must know that they should know the lines by the given date and be prepared to struggle through the rehearsals which follow with the help of the prompt, but without their own script. This should happen no later than two-thirds of the way through the rehearsal period, for actors can neither work with props nor perfect their characterisation while they are holding a script.

Once the scripts are down and moves and character are progressing well, it is a good idea to hold one rehearsal, or part of one, as a **'word bash'**. The actors sit together and without incorporating any moves they say their words quickly, concentrating on picking up cues rather than on meaning. This is when line-weakness will come to light and it is an opportunity to repeat sequences until they are correct, more quickly than would be the case during a normal rehearsal. This is something which actors working in a group situation can occasionally do themselves in another room, while you work with the others in the rehearsal space.

Anyone consistently missing a cue (and actors sometimes do find a 'blank spot' when lines just will not stay with them) may be helped if the speaker who gives the cue then tosses a soft cushion at the other as a reminder! Having at last said his line correctly, the other then tosses the cushion on to whoever speaks after him! It's a trick which is rarely needed more than once, but it does help.

A DIRECTOR'S CHECK LIST

As rehearsals begin to take shape and the moves flow, take your eyes off the script, put it down beside you and watch the action. The actors still have their books so they shouldn't make mistakes, and if they do your script is nearby for you to check. And once your prompt is beside you, you need never look at the lines unless you really need to – leave that job to her. You have more important work to do.

There are questions you must ask yourself and checks you should make as you guide your actors toward the high standards you want them to reach. Some of the questions are best not addressed to the actors themselves until their books are down, but the following checks, which are based on mistakes sometimes found in amateur drama, could make a beginning to your list if you don't already have one of your own.

1. Are the moves and groupings really effective, or should they be 'tweaked' a little to make them more interesting? Check they haven't caused any masking, by moving round the back of the hall to view the action from all angles as the scene is played out.

2. Watch the spacing – do your actors still stand too far apart in an argument or would it be better if they were closer? One aspect of an argument lies in encroaching on another's personal space. Is anyone speaking upstage or being masked? These errors generally occur because one actor is not standing in the right place, and it may need no more than a slight, almost unseen movement to correct it – (a movement called 'cheating'). It all comes down to spatial awareness (see p150).

3. Does the body language match the character's thoughts and actions? Does the actor understand the reason for the way he behaves or for what he does? Do the actors move, walk and sit in the way their character would?

4. Do the characters interact convincingly or should you help a particular actor 'find' his character by talking it through with him on a one to one basis? Would it help them all to 'hot seat' (p129) the people they are playing or improvise a short scene connected with the text at any point? As already noted, many of the activities in Section 3 are designed to help with characterisation and if you can find time these can be valuable exercises. In the short term, you

could suggest that when an actor sees people like his character in daily life, he studies them.

5. Are any actors using repetitive gestures (these can be irritating to anyone watching). Can they all stand still if they have to without fidgeting? Would that first time actor appear more confident if he were given a prop to hold? When he turns, does he turn correctly with his face toward the audience? When he has to indicate or give something, does he do so with the upstage hand and if he has to kneel, does he kneel on his downstage knee? In all cases these rules give the audience a slightly clearer view of what the actor is doing.

6. Do actors exchange eye contact? Are they working as a team? Are the relationships between the characters convincing?

7. When two actors are speaking to each other while standing face to face, can you see their expressions? If not, 'open them out'. Each actor steps back on his downstage foot, giving it a quarter turn away from his body. This turns the body very slightly towards the audience so that even though the actors are still standing in the same place, they are more accessible to anyone watching. An actor continually speaking in profile could also try this technique, if appropriate.

8. When an actor makes an exit or an entrance, is it done with intention? (see p179). For example if he is supposed to arrive with urgent news, does he appear breathless/anxious/excited? And if he must rush off, does he maintain that speed until out of sight or slow down before he reaches the wings, like a small child in a running race? And can the actors handle opening and closing doors convincingly and with aplomb?

9. Are the actors picking up their cues quickly enough? Check the delivery of the dialogue – does it have the pace/tone/emphasis which it needs to make that scene convincing? Ask the actors concerned what they are thinking or feeling as they speak.

10. Are the words clear, or is some delivery 'breathy', weak or monotonous? Can you hear all the dialogue at the back of the hall?

11. Are the 'highs' and 'lows' of the scene in the right place and do they convey the mood/emotion of the action as well as they should?

12. Perhaps the most important check of all – are the actors listening to each other, *really listening*, or do they sometimes appear to lose concentration? This really matters in the last stages of rehearsal, for if an actor has only listened for his cue, he will be nonplussed if it

is not given correctly. He may momentarily drop out of character as he struggles for the words and perhaps fail to use the correct intonation for his line. Listening is one of the keys to confident and successful acting, (and to insist on this skill may help the nervous first time actor mentioned in question 5.)

GIVING NOTES

Throughout the rehearsal period you will give many 'notes' and it can be difficult sometimes to leave the actors to make the mistakes they must make, in order to find out for themselves how something should be done. After all, that's what rehearsal is all about: trying things out. So give an actor time to find his character, for example, before leaping in with your idea of what he should be like – perhaps ask him to look again at the text and use discussion to help solve any problems which arise.

Comments on work done should, as far as possible, begin with words of encouragement before any 'notes' are given. It is always possible to find something good to say, even if occasionally it has to be something like, 'That was a good start.' Try to say something, even to the actor who is doing so well that there is little you need to say. Every actor needs to know that you have at least noticed what he is doing. Leave them all with the feeling that, although they are good, you know that they still have more to offer.

When running a section, don't stop the flow unless you have to. Write your notes down and give them when the section's finished. It's often helpful to then repeat that work incorporating the new ideas/corrections/change of pace, whatever improvements you suggested.

Avoid giving any notes after the Dress Rehearsal, unless they are essential.

TIME TO 'POLISH'

The final weeks should see 'run-throughs' of the play and they should be just that, for by now the actors should know what they are doing. Inevitably things will go wrong, but if at all possible you should resist the temptation to intervene during a run. Better that actors try to get themselves out of a situation themselves, rather than stand gasping, waiting for help. With this in mind, it's also wise to slot into the schedule one or two occasions when time may be given to those parts of the script which still need extra work.

It is also a good idea, especially with an inexperienced cast, to bring in other group members or a few friends to act as an audience for one of these run-through rehearsals. This gives the cast the chance to feel what it's like to have an audience and to experience reaction from them. It's particularly valuable if the play is a comedy, for the actors will have to remember to 'hold' their line for a beat or two when the audience laughs.

Then, too, if the venue for performance is different from that of rehearsals, at least one rehearsal or a visit by the actors and crew should be arranged during this time so that they have some idea of the stage they are to work on.

Costume

Time may have to be slotted into the schedule for trying on costume, although it is better if the initial work in this department can be done out of rehearsal time. If costumes are of a period when ladies wore long skirts, long practice skirts should be worn, since actors will have to learn how to move in them. The same rule applies to footwear, for whether period or modern, different shoes can change the way you walk. Actors should be encouraged to wear their 'performance' shoes during rehearsals because they will add to characterisation and improve movement. It is also wise, if possible, to have one rehearsal in full costume to check that it is correct, that colours blend and that no more alterations are needed. If there are to be changes they are better done at this point, rather than left until the official dress rehearsal night.

Crew

It is during these final weeks that you should see that everyone who's part of the backstage crew attends as many rehearsals as possible so that they, as well as the actors, know the play well. No-one, no matter how willing, can arrive at the last rehearsal to help with a scene change if they haven't done it before, or worse still, if they don't really know what the play is about. They will only succeed in getting in the way and slowing everything down.

Get-In

If at all possible, this should take place on the day or evening before the technical rehearsal, especially if lighting has to be rigged, for this is best done before backcloth or flats, furniture, carpets and other fittings are put in place. If previous production meetings have gone to plan, this event should not affect your acting team. they will be working with you elsewhere on any final bits of 'polish' that may be needed, although as director, you should be on stage at some time in the Get-In to check that everything is as you planned it to be. The people in charge of costume and properties as well as the crew and stage management should attend on this occasion, for everything will have to be brought in ready for use.

By the end of the Get-In the stage management team should be able to check that there are no obstacles, stray wires or frayed carpet for anyone to fall over; that supporting weights and braces used with flats are secure and marked; that there is enough blue light backstage for people to see what they are doing without it flooding into the stage area and that all tools, nails and other equipment have been put away. In other words, the area should be clean and safe before actors arrive, so that they and the technicians may begin the final stage of rehearsal. This is what the group should aim for, but it's fair to say that in very many cases, getting everything in and organised generally takes much longer than anyone imagined it would.

Technical rehearsal

If you are using the hall which you've used for rehearsals, the following point may not apply. It depends on the technical facilities you have, but if you have the opportunity – and the luxury – of working with the technicians in the performance venue before the actors arrive, you should do so. This would enable you to go through the script cue by cue, with them and the DSM if you need one, agreeing on what you want and how it can be achieved without interruption from anyone else. Even if you don't have a technical lighting rig to work with, you could finalise your sound cues at this stage (or better still during the last rehearsals) so that there'll be less to worry about during the actual 'Tech.'

On the official Tech. night, the crew should arrive as early as possible to finish putting the set and its dressing in place if this is still necessary, and the stage manager should make sure that he has allocated dressing rooms, put out coffee nearby and filled the kettle! The technical rehearsal is, as its name suggests, mainly for the benefit of the backstage workers and whoever is responsible for the sound and lighting. It is hoped, though, that technicians will already have had some input during the latter stages of rehearsal and will know what they have to do. It is also the opportunity for the actors to get to know the acting area for their performance, now that it is dressed with all the correct furniture. Before the evening's work begins, the stage manager should allow them time to find their way round the set, practise opening doors and have a 'guided tour' of the backstage area, before settling in their dressing rooms. To this end, the cast should be asked to arrive about an hour before the rehearsal begins. The time spent on this evening is especially valuable if the performance venue is different from that where rehearsals have been held.

During this evening's rehearsal it's often possible for the actors just to 'top and tail' the lines and the action, so that only lines before and after any (technical) cue are spoken. These could be linked to scene changes, exits and entrances, sound and lighting cues or anything specific which happens on stage. Actors must understand that this rehearsal is not really for them, but for the other half of the production team who only have this one opportunity to set things up correctly. Actors can sit and watch, but they should always be within calling distance in case they are needed. You may want to see what costume and make-up looks like under the lighting, but this decision may rest on how finished the set is and whether it would be wiser to keep costumes in the dressing room until work on the set is complete and paint is dry. This is when the stage manager should make sure that all the backstage crew know exactly what they are doing, although, again, they should have been practising their work during rehearsal. You will run the rehearsal along with the PM or SM, having previously marked your own script with the points at which various cues occur. If you are working in a theatre, your DSM should communicate both with you and the technicians.

There is a sequence of events which signal the beginning of the show, and this should be practised as part of this rehearsal. Once the hall doors are closed and the backstage lights have been switched off, the sequence generally runs: **a)** The signal is given for **b)** House lights to go out, and then pre-show music fades out over about 10 seconds – this should give the audience time to settle; **c)** the stage lights come up **d)** and any sound which is being used (birdsong, for example) fades in before **e)** the curtains open, not too quickly. This is repeated after the interval, which generally lasts twenty minutes. At the end of the show, the House lights come up once the final curtain has fallen, and if there is to be end-of-show music, this comes in then, too.

If at all possible, on this Tech. evening, the cast should practise how they will take the curtain call at the end of the show. This is called the 'walkdown' if the cast do literally walk downstage to applause, but however you mean the cast to line up, they need to know in advance what they should do – and if they get into place behind the end-of-act curtain, the SM must make sure that they are ready before the final curtain's drawn back. It would spoil everything if someone were to be seen scuttling in late because he'd thought he could go up to the dressing room! This will be your final bit of 'plotting' for the show, as you work out how to achieve a neat organised line up or a posed picture of the cast. It gives a professional end to the performance and leaves both actors and audience feeling pleased and satisfied. It is the detail which counts in everything that's done in the name of drama, amateur or otherwise.

Sometimes a technical rehearsal can, by its very nature, be a long one, since mistakes must be rectified and action repeated. But the actors, and you in particular, should be patient and ready to wait while technicalities are sorted out so that whatever went wrong can be re-worked correctly. It will be too late on first night.

MAKE-UP

The use of greasepaint among amateurs in the twenty-first century is rare, unless there is some special effect which can only be obtained through its use. It's a good idea for make-up to be used during the Tech so that it can be checked from the auditorium and under the correct lighting, corrected if necessary and used again for the dress rehearsal. As a general rule, unless you are working in a very large hall, ordinary, every day cosmetics, applied perhaps a little heavier than usual, or in a darker shade, with rouge, are sufficient, but tissue any stickiness off your skin before you begin. Eye shadow should not be too dark a colour, and use mascara and lipstick. The face should be powdered down with translucent powder, lightly brushed off with a downward stroke.

Men, too may need to use a foundation to maintain their natural skin colour. There can be no set rule as to which kind is best, since a great deal depends on the lighting, and so trial and error is generally the order of the day. What should be remembered is that stage lighting 'washes out' colour and only the director or others sitting in the auditorium during the technical rehearsal can judge the effectiveness of any make-up.

DRESS REHEARSAL

This should be run as a performance, in complete costume and make-up, starting at the correct performance time and with no stoppages apart from the interval. Timing should be as it will be throughout the run, from the opening sequence to the walk down, the bow and the final curtain. This rehearsal is when a photographer, if there is to be one, may be present, and actors should be warned to ignore the flash of the camera and continue with the play.

Any notes you wish to give should come at the end if they are really necessary, but remember that, by this time, anyone making a mistake will be only too aware of it and notes could make everyone even more nervous on the first night. Better that you wish the whole team good luck and cross your fingers in private!

The dress rehearsal is, by tradition, the last time that you, as director, should have any input into the production you've worked on for so long – and generally this is the night when something unforeseen is likely to happen! Indeed, theatre tradition has it that a poor dress rehearsal makes for a good first night, and if, on that first night everyone is concentrating, listening and working to the best of their ability, this will hold true. Now the stage manager is in charge, (see p90) and it is to him that actors should go if they have a problem, which he will refer to you if he is unable to solve it himself. It's now time for you to sit back, watch the fruits of your labour and, hopefully, feel justly proud of what you and the team have achieved.

FIRST NIGHT AND BEYOND

First night. Backstage, adrenaline will be high and nerves will threaten to take over, until the actors remember to take a deep breath and remind themselves that they know what they are doing. Then the play will take off and it will all happen so quickly that as they take the curtain call, some will wonder if they missed a bit somewhere. The chances are that they haven't and they will all tumble into the Bar eager to hear what the audience thought. Drinks all round and a job well done – well, *begun*, for it's not over yet.

The **second night** is, by comparison, more difficult. Relief at having done it once, together with a lower state of adrenaline will mean that the actors in particular, must maintain their concentration at a higher level if they are to achieve the high standard they reached on the first performance. Everyone must remember that this audience is seeing the play for the first time and they deserve the best which the company can give. Indeed, the group must remember this on every subsequent evening. They must never let concentration slip until the final curtain comes down, for every audience is different and is quite likely to react in a different way to each performance, but they've paid for a ticket and they deserve the best you can give.

The **last night** comes all too soon and it's unlikely that this particular team will ever perform this particular play again. Those who've been in this position before will know that next week, when the pressure's off, they will feel quite lost for a while until they've picked up the threads of normal life again. It's on the last night that the practical joker in the pack may suggest playing a joke on one of his fellow actors during performance. He should be strongly persuaded that this is not a good idea. It could easily put someone off their performance, the audience may not even notice – and if they do, many won't think it particularly funny that their enjoyment of the show has been spoiled – and at worst, the joke could backfire and cause a problem. Better to keep the production as professional as possible so that you can all leave in a haze of glory, knowing that you were successful and that your audience will return for your next show.

THE STRIKE

The euphoria will probably soon disappear when actors see how quickly their set comes down and as already noted, it's sincerely hoped that everyone lends a hand. Actors owe this to the hardworking crew, as they will realise when they take their turn backstage. Amateur drama is a team venture in every sense of the word, and very rewarding for being so … So, which play are you going to do next?

AFTER SHOW 'POST MORTEM'

Perhaps 'de-briefing' would be a better definition of the first meeting after a show. Everyone will be anxious to know what members of the audience thought and how much money's been made. If the treasurer's had time, it's best if relevant figures can be given there and then, and any other 'loose ends' tied, such as finalising the packing away and return of costume and props. This is not, however, the time for public criticism of any individual – actor, crew member or technician. The director/producer will know how different people worked or reacted to any given situation, and these thoughts he should keep to himself and bear in mind for future reference. But the important thing to remember is that there will always be something to learn from every venture. So members might consider the following –

- Did you estimate the budget correctly and have you made a profit?
- Was the event organised as well as it could have been?
- Was the publicity as effective as had been hoped? How could it be improved?
- Were there any complaints from the audience – about anything?
- Were there any unforeseen problems backstage and how could they be avoided next time?
- Were the actors confident in what they were doing, and were the characters believable? Were the actors audible at the back of the hall?
- Did any difficulties arise in any area, which should have been foreseen and should therefore be borne in mind next time?

But whatever happened, however the show went, it must be recognised that it was certainly something worth doing, and having learned whatever lessons were thrown up, the group must determine that the next show will be even more successful.

11 NOTES FOR THE ACTOR

what this chapter covers...

In this chapter we will look at some of the skills needed to produce a good on-stage performance. We start by considering character and how to find clues to what your character is *really* like from the script. We will move on to tips for learning lines before addressing some common questions beginners ask.

NOTES FOR THE ACTOR ...

Once cast in a play you, as an actor, can be sure that you'll enjoy yourself and probably learn a great deal. But you have special responsibilities and there are several things you should bear in mind. Remember that

- You have taken on a commitment and you owe it both to yourself, the director and to the other actors to attend rehearsals when required to do so and to arrive on time. Believe it or not, you will be missed if you're not there when you should be and your absence will affect everyone else's work, not just your own. You must be prepared to work as a member of the team. 'Prima donnas' are neither popular nor successful.

- Rehearsals are only the tip of the iceberg when it comes to the script. The actor who leaves his book unopened between rehearsals will never succeed. You should study the script and practise at home, perfecting the moves and learning the lines. You should think about the character you're playing until you know so much about him that you can become him.

- Once the blocking's been done, you should work at learning the lines and be prepared to drop the script when required to do so. Until now, your script has been something of a crutch, but now you must walk without it. At first you're bound to wobble, but as your steps (lines) become stronger with each rehearsal, so the wobble becomes less, until at last you're standing confident on your own two feet. For tips on how to learn lines, see p132, but whichever method you choose, do it regularly. If possible set aside some time each day – while washing up, having breakfast, before sleep, whatever time is best for you. Even when you know them, go over the lines in your head. The man in the car waiting beside you at traffic lights may wonder why you're muttering to yourself, but that matters little!

- You should always carry a pencil during rehearsal – preferably one with a rubber at the end. Always write in a move or a director's note immediately – even a bright idea about your character when it occurs to you – as well as any cuts or move changes there may be.

- You must *Listen, listen, listen!* – to the director and to the other actors. Until you listen to the full dialogue instead of just listening for your cue, you will never 'be' your character, you'll only ever be acting.

- The audience is the 'fourth wall' once you're on stage. They can see you but you mustn't try to see them, unless you're in pantomime or have to direct remarks to them. Having said that, you will be aware of them and their reactions. If you're playing comedy, you may sometimes have to pause when they laugh. With experience, you'll develop a sixth sense and the ability to connect with them. But don't stand looking to see if Uncle Jim's in the audience. Stay in character and concentrate only on your fellow actors and on what's happening around you on stage. During the performance, that stage is your only world and you should look for no other.

- Leave your day-to-day problems and any personal anxieties outside the hall door. You can do nothing about them while you're on stage. It may seem difficult advice to follow, but you owe it to yourself and to those you're working with to concentrate on the play while you're together. And having 'been someone else' for a short while, you may even return to your own life more able to cope with your worries.

Now you know all that, and you have your script (with your name on it!) you can begin. If you're like every other actor, you'll begin by flicking through the script to read all your own lines several times but none of the others – that's the first thing everyone does! Then read the whole play again, twice. Before you start work on it, you must know what it's about, what your role is within it, who the other characters are, what your relationship is to them (if any) and how the scenes are shaped to tell the story. As you read, you'll begin to understand all this. You may become so enthusiastic that, even before rehearsals begin, you may want to start learning your lines. Even though it's said that some famous directors liked their cast to come to the first rehearsal knowing their words, at this stage that's not always a good idea. By all means familiarise yourself with your lines, but don't actually commit them to memory yet, not until you really understand the exact meaning and the thoughts behind them and the context in which they're said. It's very difficult to change or re-learn a sentence if you used the wrong intonation when you first memorised it.

For now, highlight your lines with a highlighter or a red pen – and you could highlight your cues in a different colour, because it's just as important that you learn those as well. Then, having been careful to put your rehearsal schedule where you'll always see it, you're at last ready to begin rehearsal!

... AND QUESTIONS OFTEN ASKED

Even before rehearsals start, you'll begin to ask yourself some questions, and the most obvious one is:

WHO IS THIS CHARACTER I'M PLAYING?

The first thing to remember is that there's no such thing as a small part, every character in the play matters. You can make a cameo part memorable just as easily as a major role, so long as you act with truth and are convincing in everything you do and say. To find out who you are, or are going to be, you should consider

The playwright's instructions, which generally come before your first entrance. They will give you some facts on which you can build, and you'll already know where the scene takes place.

Posey stands by the French windows, holding a cup of coffee. She's a pretty girl in her twenties. She wears a rich satin housecoat and dainty slippers. She looks thoughtful and doesn't seem to notice the maid clearing the breakfast things. Clay enters. He's a heavy man in his fifties, florid, tight lipped. He's dressed in hunting pink and he holds a whip. He stares at his daughter irritably.

Now whether you're Posey or Clay you know your age, have some indication of your appearance, relationship, possible social status and of the mood you're in. Later the playwright may tell you through the dialogue that Posey's an actress or Clay is ill and because of what happens, you may have to change your original thoughts about your character. You'll certainly have to add to them, but this first description is a start. Use a notebook to jot down what you find out from the script as you read, and each time add the page number for future reference.

What other characters say about you – of Posey, for example:

If only she didn't treat everyone as if they were a fool

She's a spiteful little piece

Obviously there's more to Posey than meets the eye. Someone may say of Clay:

He used to be so generous – did you know he went bankrupt?

Perhaps this and the illness which you may be told about later go toward explaining why Clay looks bad-tempered – or perhaps on another page of dialogue you'll find out that he's just quarrelled with someone.

How your character acts/reacts to others. This you'll find out from the dialogue, too, from what you say and do as each scene is played out. To look at Posey and Clay again: as the scene progresses, we learn more about the relationship between Clay and his daughter. Here Posey stands close to her father as she talks about Arthur, the man she wants to marry.

Posey	Well, Daddy …you will be nice to him, won't you, darling – please.
Clay	Nice? To Arthur ? Why should I? Can't stand the fella.
Posey	Oh Daddy, please. I love him. We want to get married. You know, I told …
Clay	Married! To him? You marry that … that … idiot! You can forget that. It's my money he wants, my girl, not you!
Posey	Oh, Daddy! How could you! How could you! We love each other and …
Clay	Forget it, Posey. I've said no. (*Clay moves to the window*)
Posey	Forget it? Forget it? How dare you. And what do you know, anyway? I'm not a child. If I want to marry him, I will and you can't stop me.
Clay	I can and I will, just you believe it! Now, do as you're told. Go and find that so-called gardener of ours.
Posey	I won't! Find him yourself. And as soon as Arthur comes, I'm going to tell him we're leaving – now – and I'll tell him why. I'm going upstairs to pack. Just wait 'til Mother hears about this. (*Posey flounces out*)

Both characters are becoming more 'real' and this certainly adds to our initial impression of Posey – when she doesn't get her way, she loses her temper.

What you, as the character, say about yourself. Are you honest or do you hide your real feelings? Do you always tell the truth, or do you change facts in order to achieve some particular aim? As you study the text, you'll get to know your character well, especially if you stop to ask yourself *why* you're saying or doing certain things.

But once you've taken as much from the script as you can, it's time to use your imagination and ask questions of this new person that you're becoming: Who am I? What happened to me before the play began, what was I doing? How did I get to this situation and where am I going, metaphorically speaking? What do I want at any given moment in the play and what is my long term intention? Why do I want it? How am I going to achieve it and what will happen to me if I don't succeed?

Does my character change during the play? Look at other drama – Mrs Bennett in 'Pride and Prejudice', for example, was motivated in everything she did by the desire to see her daughters marry well. In 'Hobson's Choice', Willie Mossop began as a lowly boot mender and ended owning his own shop. Answer your questions in the light of what you already know from the lines you're learning and your own imagination. By the time you've worked out the answers, you will have created a much more rounded character, and you will be able to sit in a 'Hot Seat' and give convincing answers about yourself to questions which others may ask. If you don't do this analysis, you'll never really know what makes your character tick, and this you have to do if you're going to portray him truthfully – whether you like him or not.

Your characters should be real people, however unusual or strange they may be.

Don't judge them. Try to get inside their skin and understand them. And this applies when you're playing comedy, too. Think of the comic characters you've seen on stage or TV. The most successful actors believe in their characters, and they never play them for laughs. They take them seriously and play them with truth, which is why they make audiences laugh. That's the way to success.

So how do I bring him to life?

Every actor discovers for himself how he may best become another character, and as you've seen, the clues will be there for you to find.

Professional actors have their own ways of pinpointing the essence of the character. In the light of the script, some first decide on how he would dress, and with the help of the costume department, they'll find what they feel are the right shoes and coat. Actor David Suchet, on the other hand, is recorded as saying 'for me, the voice is the entry point for any character.' When portraying Sir Robert Maxwell in a television play, he deliberately deepened his voice to express Maxwell's big stature, his 'power, self assurance and incredible confidence.' Once you've studied your character, you'll make him live by:

- **Creating his physical presence.** Everybody has his own posture, his own way of moving and this can be related to his body, age, sex, mood and emotion. He may remind you of an animal or of someone you know. Posey's behaviour on the previous pages may remind you of a cat, almost purring as she tries to cajole her father into being nice to Arthur. Then, when he says 'No', she suddenly turns, claws at the ready, to spit at him in anger (metaphorically) before 'flouncing' out of the room. On the other hand, Lady Potts, her mother, is described as 'tall, angular and refined', but she's unpopular. Perhaps she looks down her nose at the world. Perhaps in some ways she's not unlike a giraffe in her posture. Watching how other people, like your character, move or behave in an every day situation may also help give you ideas as to how to create his physical presence. As you get to know more about him, as you get under his skin, you'll change your own body language to become his.

- **Speaking as he would speak.** This links closely to what sort of person you are, your attitudes, thoughts and feelings. These will reflect in the tone of your voice, the delivery of the lines, whether you speak quickly, carelessly or in a refined accent. A well-written dialogue should indicate how your character speaks, but the pace, inflection and tone of voice will come through your own study of the lines. Even minor characters can be brought to life in a few words. For example, after the murder of Lady Potts, everyone is questioned, even the neighbours, Lily and Rose, who only appeared briefly at the beginning of the first scene.

Nick   When did you last see Her Ladyship?
Lily   (*jumps*) Me? Oh, Oh dear, ... Well. When we were here, this morning ... Rose and I ... we came ... Oh dear, it's dreadful, dreadful! (*gulps*) Well, this morning we arrived ... er ... arrived early to see about the drinks, you see ... Helping, you know ... Oh, ...

Rose   Come along, Lily! Pull yourself together. (*to Nick*) We saw Delphinium straight after breakfast. Went to the kitchen with her. Would have preferred to have spoken here, not in the kitchen, but ... Well, she showed Lily what she wanted her to do and then she and I – Delphinium, I mean – went into the greenhouse to see her orchids.

Having read this aloud, how would you describe the characters of both Lily and Rose? Even these few lines show how different they are. If you want to see how other writers create character through dialogue, read 'The Doll's House' by Henrik Ibsen and note how Torvald and Nora speak to each other. Compare this with modern writers like Alan Ayckbourn and John Godber and see how they create believable characters through language.

- **Dressing as he would dress.** Actors know that what they wear will go a long way towards bringing their character to life, but don't rely on this in the beginning. You should, however, wear your character's shoes in rehearsal, for these will affect both your posture and the way you walk. Your director and wardrobe mistress will have given costume a lot of thought and they'll provide you with what they believe is right for your character. Be diplomatic in discussion with them if you don't agree! But first, work on yourself. Then costume and props should be the icing on the cake and you'll really be whoever you're meant to be.

The most important piece of advice anyone can give an actor is that the best way to find the truth of all motivation and movement is to '**People watch**'. Don't just do what you *think* people do: study them so that you *know* what they do. Watch how they move, how they behave in any given situation, how they greet a friend. See how the tramp walks and compare it with the happy child and the nervous woman, the earnest bank clerk and the brash teenager. See how the old man settles on a bench in the sun-warmed High Street and watch how carefully that pregnant woman sits down. Sit in a coffee bar or watch people as they go about their daily lives and notice how they behave. Try to work out what their occupation might be, what the relationship is to the person they're with, where they're going or where they've been – always remembering to behave discreetly yourself, of course! It can be a fascinating occupation and although you'll never know if your musings were correct, you'll certainly have a better idea of how people behave. Apply that knowledge to the character you play on stage and you will play him with *truth* – and that's the way to acting success.

How to mark up your working script

The temptation with a long speech is to try to get through it as quickly as possible, both in learning and especially in the speaking of it – and this is just about as effective as starting to knit more quickly so that you can finish a garment before the wool runs out. Before you are able to deliver a long speech effectively, with appropriate feeling, tone and pace, you must analyse it – know what's gone before, your intention (why you're saying what you say, whether you mean what you say), what you hope to achieve, if anything. If you find it difficult to phrase or even to understand the lines, you should transpose them into your own words, then you'll get the feeling of them and that will come through when you return to the scripted words. This is also a useful method of dealing with any line of dialogue which doesn't seem to convey the right meaning or 'sound right'.

As you begin to read your lines aloud, stop to pencil in notes of how you think your character feels at any given point and so how he might say them. Then, initially using the printed punctuation as a guide, pencil in the pauses along with any other pauses you use for effect (see p172). Your ideas may change as rehearsals progress, but if they do, change your script notes to match. Remember that in a long speech especially, you have a quite a lot of information to convey and the audience only has one chance to hear it. Speak as if you're talking to a friend or confidant and make what you say meaningful without labouring the point.

Opposite is an example of one way to mark a script. This is part of the dialogue between Nick Andre, Lady Potts gardener, and Heidi, the maid, who's been sent to fetch him. The actor has marked in pauses – one line for an ordinary one-beat pause, two lines for a slightly longer one. He's also marked reminders about how he should speak and how he feels, (although he'll have used pencil in case he finds his first ideas wrong.) This speech also shows the audience what sort of man Nick really is – not as subservient as he at first appeared.

Learning the lines

The second thing which might strike you once you see your dialogue high-lighted is, 'However am I going to learn all that?' The answer is, 'A section at a time' and the process will become easier as your understanding of both the plot(s) and your character grows. All the same, you're going to have to work at it, and understanding how

> **Nick** Madam wants me, does she? Oh //.. right. /I'll be there when *cross* I've finished trimming this. // All this fuss. *muttering* /I've more to do than run around ... // Rose Garden. I ask you.//I 'ad a lovely herbaceous border there, an' they all had to come out./A sin that was. / I'd put in two years solid work getting' *feels his skills not appreciated* them to flower right./'Are you sure?' I said when she told me, and she looked down 'er nose, like she does./'Roses, Andra,'/ *mimics LP* she said. 'We're having a new Rose Garden there. See to it.'/Just like that. 'See to it.'/I've worked this garden all me life, *bitterly* an' to be told .../Oh, alright, girl, stop 'oppin' *impatiently* from one foot to t'other. I'm coming /and I aint washin' me 'ands neither. I've work to do. *stamps off to greenhouse*

Fig 13. How to mark up a script.

memory itself works can help you to decide which learning techniques are best for you.

Memory lives in the whole of the brain, which has definite areas for visual and auditory stimulus and for association. So, for example, the 'visual' area stores the printed word and its associations – and where this is particularly strong someone is said to have a 'photographic' memory. The 'auditory' area of the brain recognises sounds in speech, while that part of the brain controlling the mechanical, muscular activities of the tongue and throat are responsible for speech itself. The centre concerned with muscular control of the hand remembers the physical act of writing.

So, when learning lines, more than one area of the brain can and should be used –

1. **Visual.** (seeing your lines) – a) recalling the shape of the text and the lines themselves, where they are on the page. You can also employ some of the tricks we use to help the memory – like b) the shape of words. It's well known that children learning to read will recognise the word 'elephant' more easily than 'can' or 'man'.

c) Remembering the alphabetical position of the first or second letters of words – for example, Posey's lawyer friend Arthur has to say he had to change a car tyre and then two or three speeches later he has to mention the wheel, but the actor playing him can't remember in which order the comments come. Remembering that in the alphabet T comes before W will help him get it right. d) Using mnemonics can help, too, as in remembering the order of the colours of the rainbow (**R**ichard **O**f **Y**ork **G**ave **B**attle **I**n **V**ain – **r**ed, **o**range, **y**ellow, **g**reen, **b**lue, **i**ndigo, **v**iolet))

2. **Auditory.** (hearing your lines). Read them aloud. Ask someone to give you the cues and say your lines aloud. Record them and play them back or just record the cues and speak your words. Keep the tape or disc in your car and play it as you drive. Noticing any alliteration in a line can help – 'We must hope for client confidentiality' is another scripted line for Arthur. But in rehearsal the actor kept saying 'client discretion', though he knew it was wrong. Then, saying the words aloud, he noticed that the correct word, 'confidentiality' begins with the same letter as 'client'. Then he remembered the line correctly. Perhaps when learning, you could speak (in your head) a rhyme, which reminds you of the word or phrase you have to remember, and then say it.

3. **Association.** Link lines, phrases or words with something which is already familiar to you.

4. **Mechanical memory** (the physical use of associated muscles) by –
   a) physically writing or typing out the lines you must learn, more than once, if necessary – and this, of course links with visual association;
   b) speaking the lines aloud as you learn them or even singing them, which links with auditory memory.

Using a variety of methods, and perhaps all four, will not only make the necessary home study of your lines more interesting, it will also make the process easier as you discover which method works best for you. Then, if you want to know if you really know your part, ask someone to give you your cue from anywhere in the play, or write out the cues and pick one out at random and see if you can reply correctly. Many professional actors can do it, and you could too!

MORE TIPS

Divide the work into short periods rather than one long session. Learn a page or two at a time, and don't move on to a new section too quickly.

Study regularly and at a time when it won't be followed by strenuous mental work. Try to follow a learning session by a routine physical task – the washing up or a brisk walk. Some prefer to study a script during breakfast, others do so before going to bed. You'll soon find what works best for you.

If you have to learn a long speech, analyse it before you begin to memorise it, so that you know exactly what it's all about. Read it a few times and pay attention to the punctuation. This is your guide. Then mark where the different thoughts come, think about what your character's saying, how his thoughts and/or mood changes. Mark where you might change your tone of voice or timing to match those different thoughts or feelings in the speech, and mark in pauses where you'll need to take a breath. Then, when you know what you're saying and why you're saying it, speak it aloud and listen. Does it make sense now? If it does, memorising that speech will be much easier.

Your memory will go on working even when you've consciously finished with it – why else can we recall a piece of music more easily the day after we've heard it, than immediately after hearing it?

Forgetting comes through interference, suppression, or lack of interest in what we should remember – or through lack of concentration and the will to learn in the first place. The moral is, therefore, that anyone, especially in this case, the actor, should enjoy what he's doing and really want to do it!

OTHER QUESTIONS ACTORS SOMETIMES ASK

DOES IT MATTER IF I DON'T LEARN THE EXACT WORDS?

Yes, it does, for two reasons.

1. The writer chose his words with care, often writing and re-writing them several times until they convey his exact meaning. They'll also have a rhythm which makes the lines flow smoothly. If you change them, the nuance of meaning could change and the fluidity of the lines will be lost, so that they 'limp' and won't sound right.

2. When you paraphrase, there's no guarantee that your speech will end with the words which the next actor's waiting for as his cue, and that could confuse him. Giving and receiving the correct cue is important in the teamwork that is drama.

HOW CAN I SPEAK SO THAT THE PERSON AT THE BACK WILL HEAR ME?

Never shout! Voice projection comes through relaxation, correct breathing and an inner confidence, which in turn comes from knowing that you're sure of what you're going to say – in this case, your lines. This can only come through a study of the script, rehearsal and practice at home. Relax your shoulder and neck muscles, learn to breathe correctly, be sure of your lines and confident that what you're about to say and do is important, (see relaxation and breathing exercises in section3). Sometimes imagining that your audience is actually behind you and not in front, can help you project your voice, but this is only a short-cut to the true skill of projection.

WHAT SHALL I DO IF I FORGET MY LINES?

Try to keep talking, say something relevant even if they're not the right words (the audience doesn't know the script anyway) and hope that the person with the next line, or the prompt is able to bring the dialogue back into focus. This should be possible if you've been working as a close team, especially if the prompt kept quiet during one or two of the rehearsals. Try not to stand there looking blank and terrified – that makes the lapse more obvious. Whatever happens, remember that other actors have done the same thing and you'll never make the same mistake again – just concentrate and listen to the others more carefully next time!

DOES IT MATTER IF I HAVE MY BACK TO THE AUDIENCE WHEN I SPEAK?

This is something best avoided. If your director has blocked the moves correctly, it shouldn't happen, unless he's deliberately plotted it that way – as he might do, if you're looking upstage to a royal figure or a deity, for example. Speaking upstage means that your voice is directed away from the audience and so you'll have to be careful to speak more clearly and project more. This could have the effect of hardening your delivery and shades of meaning could be lost, as well as your facial expression. Talking to someone upstage of you has the same disadvantage and is something to be aware of. Should this happen because you or another actor has not moved far enough or at the correct angle, one of you should 'cheat' by moving slightly as you speak so that you're more or less on a level with each other for the rest of the speech.

WHAT SHOULD I DO WITH MY HANDS? / HOW DO I STAND STILL FOR A LONG TIME?

In your daily life this is something you never think about, and if you're part of the action in a scene, then your body language will automatically solve the problem. But there are times when you just have to stand and watch and listen – and therein lies the secret. Concentrate on what's happening on stage and listen all the time. You should become so immersed in the scene that you'll forget yourself. You'll even forget that you have hands and that you're doing nothing. Your director may also be able to help a little by giving you a prop to hold or by suggesting that you lean against something. But the real answer lies in your own ability to forget yourself and concentrate on something else – in this case, your fellow actors.

How soon can I use 'properties'?

Holding props is difficult, if not impossible, when you're still holding your script, so at that stage you should just make a mental note of what you'll be doing/holding at that particular moment. Once your script is down, the props will appear, even if they're only 'rehearsal' props. Then you can learn to handle them and practice fitting the actions to the lines, which by then, of course, you'll know well.

How do I express emotions like shock or grief convincingly?

At one time or another, most actors will have experienced many of the feelings which their character must show. Happiness or joy is easy to portray, but sadness is not. Study that moment in the play quietly, by yourself, and think back to a time in your life when you experienced something like that. Try to recall how you felt and pinpoint your emotions. Read that part of the script again and as you say the lines, superimpose those emotions, which are still in your memory, but be clinical about it, don't allow yourself to be overcome by them. Repeat the exercise and say the scripted lines aloud. Listen to yourself, notice if your body moves in any particular way and remember this. Say the lines again using that vocal expression and body language, but don't think about the original occasion when you felt like that. Instead, concentrate on what your character is saying. Having done this during your private study, you should find that you'll be able to pace your lines and pitch your voice to convey those feelings on stage without actually feeling your original pain. And the more practice you have, the easier it will become.

How can I overcome first-night nerves?

Every actor has them, whether he's professional or amateur. But once you're on stage, you know that the adrenaline that goes with them will give you the energy to go ahead and act, as it does in any tense situation. So you must apply reason to your fear. You know your role, you know the lines and what you have to do, and it's very likely that most members of the audience either couldn't, or wouldn't dare, act on stage as you're about to do. They'll want you to succeed and if you make a mistake it won't be the end of the world. So in effect, there's nothing to worry about, you feel anxious only because you're human. But to help you conquer those nerves,

1. Give yourself time to settle by arriving early. Rushing in at the last minute will make matters worse. Slowly check that everything you need, costume and props, is in place and as they should be and then get ready in your own time.

2. Spend the last ten minutes before curtain up calming yourself in whatever way is best for you. If you want to warm up vocally or physically, do it now. If you need quiet, find a corner and tell the others to leave you alone. You won't be the only one who feels that the chatter of a dressing room can be too much, and a good actor should always respect another's privacy.

3. Breathe deeply and relax – put your head out of the window and take in fresh air if you want to. Physically relax and think of your character, feel who you'll be once on stage, but resist the temptation to read the script. You do know the lines now and to re-read them will confuse you – honest! Concentrate instead on centring yourself until you feel relaxed and then hold on to this feeling even in the wings. Listen to the onstage action, get ready, then as you make your entrance, switch on your energy, let your acting take over, and you've made it!

WHY CAN'T I GO FOH IN COSTUME AND MAKE-UP?

Well, of course you can, but not if you want to be professional about your acting. Professionals never appear in costume or make-up during or after a show unless it's plotted as part of the action, and doing so says 'amateur' with a capital A. You and your team have worked hard to produce a show to the highest standard you can reach, so be proud of your efforts. Stay 'professional' and don't break the spell of your performance on stage or the magic that is theatre.

SECTION 3

ACQUIRING SKILLS AND CONFIDENCE

12 PRACTICAL SKILLS

what this chapter covers...

This chapter forms an introduction to a series of chapters dealing with the practical side of drama group meetings. The games and exercises which follow form the backbone of such meetings, and are designed to be both fun and invaluable for developing the skills needed for performance.

ACQUIRING SKILLS – AN INTRODUCTION

In this section we look at activities which can be used by members of all ages in any amateur drama group, activities which are not only fun to do, but which will also help those involved to grow in confidence as well as in drama skills. As they share these activities, members will get to know each other better and learn to trust each other, and at the same time build a confidence, which will enable them to try something new and succeed in it. In particular, these exercises and improvisations should help an amateur actor learn techniques which will help improve his performance on stage. A good actor needs to know how to use concentration, imagination and observation if he is to succeed. He must be able to use both physical and vocal expression to good effect, to enjoy working as a member of a team, sharing ideas, summoning the confidence and energy to bring a written character to life. The activities in this section will foster these skills, but above all, all members of a social drama group should find that if they take part, even if just for enjoyment, they will still benefit in some way.

The following chapters should also help a drama leader to fashion an entertaining evening for members of his group. The ideas can be mixed and matched so as to provide fun, as well as perhaps targeting a particular area of expertise or skill needed in a current or forthcoming production, although only the organiser may be aware of this objective. It is expected that members will be asked to 'show' what they've done, especially in partner or group work (and especially if the leader has seen that it's good), but no member should be forced to do so if he feels his work isn't ready for 'performance'. Some activities lend themselves to this better than others, and there's not always sufficient time for a great deal of 'showing', but a group pleased with its efforts will want to share their work with fellow members. This should be encouraged, for it's an opportunity to illustrate not only individual growth, but also the ability to work in partnership with others, and it provides an opportunity for positive discussion and mutual enjoyment.

Throughout, the instructions are given as if to the individual so that they may be taken by one person, or used by a leader.

TIPS FOR THE LEADER

Do make sure, especially with a new group, that all the activities you choose to do are suitable for the membership. However enthusiastic you are, you must expect a certain amount of reticence from some members, especially if at first they don't see the point of what they're being asked to do, or feel that they're being asked to do something which might show them in an unfavourable light. It's unlikely, for instance, that men in a prison group would co-operate if you began by introducing 'Little Peter Rabbit' as a warm-up or concentration exercise! Show understanding, don't coerce, and gradually, as trust and confidence build, everyone will want to join in and you can become more ambitious.

Plan ahead and make sure that you have beside you enough material or ideas to fill the time. Know what you hope to do in any one session. It's better to have too much material than not enough, for an activity may not work as you'd thought it would and so may you may need an alternative exercise. Be aware of how much time you intend to give to each activity but be prepared to be flexible. Timing does get easier with practice, especially as the group consolidates.

Never give instructions until members are quiet and ready to listen. They should also be reminded to listen for your voice as they work, so that they don't miss further instructions. After all, listening is one of the most important aspects of stage work.

CHOOSING 'TEAMS'

As leader you may often find when you call for individual members to form couples or small groups that, like children playing team games, the same people will come together each time, but this negates the idea of learning to work with someone else, whoever he may be. Although it's to be expected that friend will partner friend at first, there are several ways of making sure that this doesn't happen on a regular basis to the exclusion of someone who may be reticent or new to the group. If you do use any of the following suggestions, don't explain why you're asking members to do as you ask. Make it more of a '*how quickly can you…*' game so that in the scramble to get into position, any barriers will be swept away by the desire to succeed. Once you've arranged the group as you wish, you can then proceed with whatever activity you had in mind.

For a **partnered activity** individuals could be asked to line up in order of height or birth month or in alphabetical order of the initial of their first name or surname, for example. Once in line, you can then move them into two lines so that each is facing someone who will be his partner – or 'cut' the lines into the group numbers you want.

As members move round the room at the end of an individual exercise, you could demand that they quickly form a **group** (of whatever number is required) by joining with those immediately nearest to them, or with those who are wearing the same colour, live in the same street, have the same eye or hair colour or shoe size, have the same birth month, had toast for breakfast – whatever you're able to choose through your knowledge of the membership. Very soon, everyone will become used to working with everyone else, new friendships will grow and all members will feel secure and a true member of a happy social group – which, after all, was one of the aims of the steering committee in the first place.

The order and choice of work from any section is obviously down to personal preference.

13 WARM-UPS

what this chapter covers…

In this chapter we explore some games which will prove valuable in both the early days of your drama group (to get members familiar with each other) and later on in preparing participants for more 'in depth' work.

…ALSO KNOWN AS ICE-BREAKERS

These activities are very useful as a way of breaking the ice for members of a newly formed group, as well as bringing members together at the start of a meeting. They foster friendship and a willingness to join in and be part of the group in whatever it may be doing next. This is especially true if the leader introduces the activity in a spirit of fun and, at first, joins in himself. In many cases these activities do also literally 'warm up' participants – especially on a winter evening – loosening up their muscles and relaxing them. So, warm-ups are valuable in that they not only relax the members physically, but they help concentration and create a friendly cohesion within the group, and this cohesion will carry through to other activities and even into stage performance.

Below is a selection of ideas which have proved to be successful, but of course you'll only use those which you consider most suitable for your group and the space they are in. These activities will, hopefully, prove a springboard for other ideas you may have.

Physical warm ups should generally be used one at a time, or two at the most, and never extended to the onset of boredom – or exhaustion! Another separate exercise, physical or vocal (a concentration or relaxation game perhaps) could follow before embarking on the main activity for the evening.

At all times you should be in control and aware of whether the exercises are being enjoyed or not.

CIRCLE GAMES

You could try 'The Hokey Kokey' dance, of course, or where music is available, The Twist, or a traditional circle dance as a 'warm-up' exercise, but the following are great ice-breakers. These too require music (piano or recorded) in the form of either a march or a jaunty tune. If no music is available everyone could sing or hum a song which they all know, as they walk or march, while you call out the changes.

CIRCLE CHAT

Members are asked to form two lines of equal numbers, so that each member is standing behind or in front of another.

Each line breaks to form its own circle **A** and **B**, one inside the other, members **A** facing someone in **B**.

Music begins: those in **A** walk round to their left, **B** to their right.

After a short interval the music stops and each member turns to the member opposite him in the other circle to exchange a remark, whatever comes into their heads – it could be anything from 'My names is …' to 'What on earth are we doing this for?'

The exercise is repeated quickly several times, with circles occasionally being asked to change direction as well. Variations can be used when, for example, instead of a random remark, members are asked to name their favourite food or television programme, what they had for breakfast or where they were born – anything as long as it's not too personal or invasive.

CIRCLE CHANGE

Circles as before, but when the music stops, and on the command 'change', members in **A** and **B** change places quickly, without speaking, so that they're in the other circle.

1. At first they continue to move in the direction of those in their new circle (ie, the opposite direction to that which they were originally moving in). Repeat two or three times, each time changing from inner to outer circle. The more frequent the 'change' call, the more fun it creates.

2. Repeat the above but command that they change circles **and** that each circle changes direction. NB. Don't allow members too long to change places, and again make the changes frequent. This will then involve another acting skill, *concentration*!

Circle Chain

While standing in two-circle formation as above, everyone from circle **A** moves to stand to the right of his opposite number in **B**.

Then each **A** and **B** face each other and touch right hands. As the music starts, all move round in the direction they face in a circle chain, first touching right hands with the person they meet and then left alternately, always moving forward, until everyone can move fluently. Stop.

Repeat the chain. This time, without stopping the flow or the music the leader commands, several times, that everyone turns to walk in the opposite direction. Few manage this without a muddle and laughter!

Circle Dance

The group surrounds one in the middle who repeats a single repetitive step – in time to the music if it is being used – a dance step which everyone else must copy. At your signal, the centre member changes places with whosoever he chooses, who must then in turn continue the 'dance' by inventing another repetitive movement for all to copy.

The circle could be broken into line by your calling out a member's name. He must then lead the group into the 'follow my leader' game, using different movements until you call for him to lead them to a halt, when the 'leader' is changed, or they return to their seats.

SPACE ACTIVITIES

These are activities introduced after each member has found a space in the room to stand in. When he is on stage, an actor should be aware of the space he occupies in relation to the others he is working with, so that he neither masks another, nor has to make a move to avoid him because he has misjudged a spatial area. These exercises, as they progress, help spatial awareness. The first two games are most suitable for young members, for they are very energetic, but even then, care should be taken if they're working on a slippery floor.

Stick in the Mud

This is a chasing game, with one member chosen as 'tag'. On the word *go* the 'tag' member tries to touch as many of the others as he can, so sticking them to the spot. They must stand still until another member frees them by tapping them on the shoulder. After a few minutes, stop and repeat with a different member tagging. The winner after two or three bouts is the 'tagger' who had the most members frozen to the spot when the game finally ends.

TAILS

Each member needs a ribbon, which can be tucked at the waist like a tail. Having found a space and on the command Go, they chase each other round the room, collecting as many 'tails' as they can until they hear 'stop'. Then the winner is the one who holds the most tails.

Standing Warm-ups, such as physical training exercise (of the 'arms stretch, knees bend' type) can be done if you have a particularly young and energetic group, but the most successful 'ice-breakers' are activities which are used as games.

SPACE AND IMAGINATION ACTIVITIES

INDIVIDUAL

THE BALL

(If the working space is small, this may have to be carried out by a few members at a time.)

In your own space, climb into a big, opaque imaginary ball. Feel the base under your feet, push your hands out against the front and sides of the ball.

You can see where you want to go, but the ball is heavy, so you'll need to push hard to roll away and round the room. Push, feel your body strain. Once you get going, it will be easier, you'll move along more quickly – but be careful not to roll into anyone else.

Keep moving, hands outstretched, keep pushing until you find a big space near the wall where you can stop moving. Rest, then climb out of the ball and find a chair or a space on the floor and sit and relax.

TOYTOWN

1. Stand in a space and imagine you're a wind-up toy. Think how you would move. Now, hold the key, and hear the sounds as you wind

yourself up. Now, off you go, demonstrating your movement. After a minute or two, the leader says, '*You're winding down now, slower, slower, and stop.*'

[2] Repeat – only after a few seconds, react as the leader says '*Oh, there's something wrong – you're going faster – and faster – oh, it's alright, the spring is slowing again – normal speed, slow down – and stop.*'

[3] Repeat once more, only this time, the speeding up results in an explosion and the toy is broken. How are you going to show this physically?

MENAGERIE

[1] Find a space and imagine you are an animal, but don't say what it is. If you are a bear, are you fierce or cuddly? Are you a showy peacock, a monkey, a shy and gentle deer, or a heavy and ponderous elephant?

Think yourself into his body and then on the command '*Go*', move about, noticing how you walk and how parts of your body move. Be aware of your paws, your tail, how heavy or strong you are. Be that animal as you move **silently** round the room trying to find others like you, animals with the same movement and body language, then sit, stand or lie beside them making your own little group, but still don't make any noise.

[2] Before you repeat the exercise, you may decide to change and become another creature. How differently will you move? This time, think how you would **communicate** as well. Which other animal might be your friend or enemy? Move round as before, only now add some form of communication – it may be a sound or a movement – as you pass other animals.

When at last you find another of your kind, stand or sit with them and hold a vocal 'conversation' in your animal language.

MOOD WALK

Stand in a space and imagine a mood which you might be in – happy, sad, excited, angry, nervous, bored, cheerful. Walk round by yourself, in any direction, but as you pass someone greet him, still in that mood; then move on, pass three more people before stopping again to talk to them, still exhibiting the mood you chose.

Repeat once more beginning in the same mood, but on the order '*Stop*' each of you should slowly turn a complete circle in your own space. As you do so, you must change your mood completely, before setting off on the exercise again.

Mood Walk Variation

This time, not showing a mood, but a physical change from you as you really are, you're about to move around the room again. Perhaps you're drunk, or carrying a heavy weight, perhaps you've injured a part of your body, or you have poor eyesight, perhaps you're pregnant or have a wooden leg, perhaps you're very old or a child going to a party – just think how you would move.

1. On the word '*Go*' set off, sensing the physical changes you've made to yourself. Do they make you want to be alone in your own space, or do you want to meet people?
2. Repeat your walk, but on the command '*Stop*', say something to the person nearest to you. Can you carry on a conversation with that person?

High and Low

These are status games, which can give some insight into the feelings and body language of characters at different social levels.

1. Everyone is given a playing card. (If cards are not available, members imagine their status as being either 'high' or 'low'). The number on the card rates your status in life, but don't tell anyone else what it is – thus 9 is of a higher status than the ace, which counts as one, and the face cards are even more 'important'. Move round the room, your body and your greeting to anyone you pass showing your status and how you view others around you. On '*stop*' hold a conversation, still in status, with the nearest member.
2. Now change your status – from high to low and vice versa – before you repeat the walk. Note the changes in both your feelings and the physical expression of them. Did you find that 'high status' stands tall, walks smoothly and has controlled speech, while 'low status' curls in on himself as if afraid and moves quickly, almost avoiding contact with others? You may find status relates to a character you play at some time. Which did you prefer? Why?
3. Imagine you are someone else, fact or fiction, either popular or unpopular for whatever reason. Your character can be contemporary or historical, as long as you know something about them.

Move round the room looking at others in the way you think your character might do, and remembering to move as he/she might. The leader should then call '*stop*', approach one 'character' and hold a conversation with him. The other members try to work out who the leader is talking to. Repeat.

PARTNER/GROUP SPACE ACTIVITIES

These activities will encourage the use of imagination and a spirit of trust and co-operation among the players. On stage, trust and co-operation are most important among actors, as is an awareness of what everyone else around you is doing. During the following games both partners and groups must be aware of the space they occupy, so as to avoid crashing into others, and use their individual spatial awareness to co-ordinate the timing with the other players in their particular game. In the 'Invisible' Games 1 and 2, everyone must 'see' and 'feel' the items they use to play their game. In fact no props may be used in any of the activities in this section. Participants should work so convincingly that anyone watching will 'see' the ball or the rope or whatever it may be, know where it is and be able to link it with the reaction of whoever receives it next.

PARTNERS

INVISIBLE GAMES 1

In a space, imagine that you're playing tennis or badminton, miniature golf, croquet, ping pong, hopscotch, tiddleywinks, marbles, outdoor (ie large enough to walk round) chess, draughts, any game which two can play, but only you and your partner know what the game is.

The leader may stop the action so that some of the partners can 'play' while others guess the game – just how convincing were the actions and was the space awareness right? Repeat.

AIRCRAFT

This game in particular incorporates trust and concentration. Members form partners **A** and **B**. **A** closes his eyes and holds his arms out to simulate an aircraft. **B** must then walk behind him, lightly touching one shoulder, guiding him round the room, speaking quietly only the words '*left*', '*right*' '*forward*', and '*stop*' until they reach their chosen destination across the room.

Then **B** becomes the aircraft and the exercise is repeated.

This can be made more difficult and requires more concentration if the guide stands at the destination to call out his instructions, but in this case, the exercise should only be carried out by a few couples at a time to avoid accidents.

CROSSING THE BRIDGE

1. Each member **A** takes a partner **B** and stands facing him across the width of the room.

   A chair or some form of marker is then placed at either end of the two lines of players, about a metre in front of them. These indicate the beginning and end of very narrow (imaginary) bridges over a deep ravine between each of the couples.

   A and **B** then set off at the same time, walking to change places with his partner – but they meet in the middle of their narrow, rickety bridge and each must cross the other to reach his destination without falling into the ravine.

2. Begin this time with each couple (**A** and **B**) on the same side of the 'bridge', which they must cross one at a time because it will not take the weight of two.

   A, who is brave, slowly and carefully crosses first. **B** sets off, but once on the bridge, loses courage. **A**, without leaving his place on the far bank, must encourage him to come across safely and successfully. Return across the bridge with **A** and **B** changing character.

Fig 14. "It's OK... just a few more steps..."

IN GROUPS

Divide players into groups of four, five or six.

HOLD IT!

Form Shapes or Tableaux – square, circle, oblong, triangle etc – or a tableau – dance finale, war memorial, copse of trees, wedding photo, christening, monkey family etc, freezing in position when asked to do so, so that others may see their interpretation.

INVISIBLE GAMES 2

Each group must act out one of the following imagining, but not actually having the equipment they need. All can practice first then each group could show their game.

a) **Skipping.** Two hold and turn a rope while the others skip in unison, or enter and leave the skipping line in turn

b) **Team Games.** A ball is passed under or over from whoever headed the team to the last in the line. He then runs to the front to repeat the exercise until the original leader is in place again.

Other team games known to members may be used to provide variety, if they require some invisible item – hoop, bean-bag etc..

c) **Tug of war with another group**.

Were the actions done properly and were they believable?

FORM A MACHINE

Each member of a group imagines himself to be part of a large machine or a cog in one, performing the repetitive movement which that part does. The 'cogs' then come together to work out the machine's continuous pattern of movements into a complete, repeated routine – First, **A**, silently and then **B** while incorporating appropriate vocal sound effects.

Fig 15. Machine!

Rituals

Each group works out a rhythmic pattern of movements and sound, which together will make up a ritual. Choose from one of the following:

- Rain Dance
- Welcoming Ceremony
- Haka
- Sacrifice
- Coming of Age Initiation
- Wedding
- Red Indian Pow-wow
- Secret Society Initiation

In no case should props be used. Knowing that the results will be shown will promote teamwork, confidence and a pooling of ideas among the groups.

Fig 16. Haka!

Furnishing

This is as more difficult exercise which could take some time! Each group is to furnish a kitchen and they must know where the 'walls' are which form their kitchen area, but they mustn't be physically marked out. Each member chooses one item found in a kitchen – large or small and it may take two to carry it. Then in turn, they carry their item into the space, (remembering its size and weight) setting it in a logical place, until the kitchen is furnished. The task is to remember exactly where the 'walls' are (and the door, of course) to mime how each item is carried in and to remember where everything has been placed. After a practice run, each group performs their 'furnishing' in front of the others, who can judge whether their collective imagination and spatial awareness is effective!

The kitchen can then be dismantled, each item in turn, if members can remember what and where they are. **NB**: It is requires even more concentration if another team has to be the 'furniture removers'.

14 CONCENTRATE!

> **what this chapter covers...**
>
> In this chapter we consider the value of good concentration, and begin to develop techniques to enable performers to do it in the most challenging of situations – on stage and under the glare of an audience...

THE NEED FOR CONCENTRATION

Concentration is an individual skill, one which everyone uses to some degree every day (and especially when acting) but it is a skill which becomes easier with practice. Most of the exercises and activities in this section incorporate some concentration, but the following are specifically designed with this in mind. So, although they may be listed as partner or group work, everyone in fact will be practising the art. Although listed under a specific heading, concentration games could also be used as warm-ups or ice-breakers or before relaxation exercises. Relaxation is generally more effective if it follows tension – and intense concentration does involve a certain amount of both mental and physical tension, even if we may not recognise it at the time. On the other hand, it could be said that people concentrate better if they are relaxed. Whatever your view, there are benefits in either case.

PARTNERS

In the first three exercises the roles should be reversed after a few minutes.

MIRROR IMAGE

This is one of the more well-known exercises. **A** and **B** stand facing each other. **A** then slowly makes movements which **B** must mirror, whether they are physical and/or facial. They may become more complicated, but they must be mirrored accurately. This can be extended into the more difficult:

Puppets

A becomes the puppet and **B** the puppeteer, who stands in front of him manipulating the strings which cause him to move.

First they must decide which hand controls the strings for which part of the body – head, arms or feet. The test of concentration lies in being able to co-ordinate the relationship between the hands which hold the strings and the reactive movement. The puppeteer must also be careful to create movements which are physically possible!

Before the change-over, each puppeteer should move his puppet into the space where he's to be stored.

Shadow Dancing

This encourages partners to be aware of each other and the space they each occupy.

A and **B** stand back to back, with **A** being the 'leader'. Still back to back but without actually touching each other, **A** should create a series of simple movements, which his partner must sense and follow. Any noise in the room will hinder concentration, so making this impossible to do.

Chatter, chatter 1

A and **B**, who sit facing each other, decide on a topic of conversation. At the signal they begin to converse for a minute.

When stopped they turn to sit back to back. **A** is asked 4 questions about his partner which he must answer without looking at him – eg what colour are **B**'s eyes/jacket/shoes/skirt/trousers/hair. Describe his face/tie, is he wearing a watch/jewellery/glasses etc.

Where did the concentration lie – in the conversation or the partner? When the exercise is repeated, the questions should be different.

Chatter, chatter 2

A and **B** sit facing each other. Each thinks of a subject on which he can speak for one minute. At the signal they both talk at the same time without pausing to listen to each other, until the call to stop.

They are then asked if they know what the other was saying and if they found they could listen without losing the thread of what they themselves were saying – something which does require concentration.

ANATOMY

A and **B** stand facing each other. **A** says 'This is my nose', but he touches another part of his body eg his knee. **B** replies by saying, 'This is my knee' while pointing to a *different* part of his body.

Each time the phrase, 'This is my …' refers to the part of the body **last** touched, but the player must touch or point to another part of his anatomy. Many people find this very difficult and it certainly tests one's powers of concentration!

IN GROUPS

PETER RABBIT

This is included for young members of a group, or for adults who have a silly sense of humour and know each other well! A movement is made for each word or phrase. If someone knows the tune, so much the better – thus

Little	*pat the knees once with both hands*
Peter	*hands held out in front, level with the shoulders*
Rabbit	*hands form ears on either side of the head*
Had a flea	*snap fingers once*
Upon his ear	*point to the right ear.*

　　Repeat these four lines three times – then

So he flicked it and he flicked it	*snap fingers right and left hand*
Until it flew away	*arms to side making flying movements.*

This may be considered too silly to do, but it's not as easy as it looks (especially if it's speeded up the second time). It does need concentration and it always causes laughter!

CHAIN REACTION

Players sit round in a circle placing both hands on a table in front of them, crossing each hand with the player on either side. Thus, your left hand should be in front of the player on your left and their right hand should be in front of you. Your right hand should be in front of the person on your right and their left hand in front of you.

To begin: One person slaps one of his hands on the table and this slap is then repeated by the next hand on his left, and so it continues round the group.

When the circle is completed, repeat the action, beginning with a new person and moving round to the right. Concentration is needed if you are to keep the rhythm going, especially when the movements are speeded up.

MOVING NUMBERS

Members sit in a circle or a line and each says a number in order, beginning at one. They must keep their number throughout the game.

- **1** The leader then calls out two numbers at random and those players change places – 7 and 12; 3 and 8; 15 and 4 etc.

  Repeat several times.

- **2** The leader calls out two numbers as before, but after that, the *higher* of the two numbers called must call another number and change places with him each time.

FIZZ – BUZZ

Stage 1. Players sit in a circle and begin counting round in order from 1, but when 5 or any multiple of 5 is reached, the player must say *buzz* instead and then the counting continues round the group.

Stage 2. When players are used to this, count as before, still using *buzz* for 5 and its multiples, but now add the word *fizz* for 7 and any multiple of 7.

So counting will begin 1 2 3 4 *buzz* 6 *fizz* 8 9 *buzz* – and so on.

Anyone failing or hesitating is not using enough concentration – and what happens when you reach 35?

ONE IS KING

This requires great concentration and it involves clapping to an 8 beat rhythm, so it's best to practice that first, step by step.

- To 4 beats, pat the knees twice and clap hands twice and repeat this (8 beats) (ie, *pat, pat, clap, clap, pat, pat, clap, clap*). Repeat these eight beats until all are familiar with the pattern.

- These actions are then repeated as spoken numbers are added over the 1st and 2nd, 5th and 6th beats: eg, if using the numbers one and eight the sequence would be *one, one, –, –, eight, eight, –, –*. That is, every time you pat your knee, a number is spoken.

The basic sequence in this example would be:

'one	one	–	–	eight	eight	–	– '
pat	pat	clap	clap	pat	pat	clap	clap

When this is understood, the players number along the line beginning at one end with the number **One**, and they keep this number as their own. Number **One** is King and he begins the game.

1. He says his number – '*one, one*' as everyone pats out beats 1 and 2 with him, and then everyone claps for beats 3 and 4.

    Then, while all pat out beats 5 and 6 '**One**' calls out another random number – *Ten, Ten* for example, and all clap hands for beats 7 and 8.

2. Whoever is **Ten**, repeats his own number (*Ten, Ten*) as the rhythm line begins again (beats 1 and 2); claps on 3 and 4; then on beats 5 and 6 he calls out *another* number – eg *Seven, Seven* – before all clap the final beats 7 and 8.

3. Number **Seven** then begins the round again by calling out his own number, and so the game continues. Anyone making a mistake must drop out.

It is best to begin slowly, because this game requires much concentration – and don't give up after the first attempt! Try it again over the weeks and everyone will be so accomplished that you can move on to...

ADVANCE THE KING

The game becomes even more challenging if the person who makes a mistake goes to the end of the line, thereby making everyone move up one place and change their number. Whoever is seated in the original number **One** chair when the game ends, is the winner.

15 RELAX...

what this chapter covers...

In the last chapter we looked at the importance of concentration. Closely allied to this is the ability to relax – a relaxed mind concentrates better than a tense one. Since mind and body work together, we will look now at effective ways to relax the body without the need for any complicated or specialised techniques.

THE NEED FOR RELAXATION

The ability to relax is of paramount importance to an actor because body tension affects both movement and voice in a negative way. No actor can work freely and with conviction if his body or mind is tense, for muscles tighten when they should relax and the mind no longer functions efficiently.

Relaxation is an individual, personal skill but it should be practised regularly so that the relaxed state can be called up easily when it is needed – as in the moments just before performance. Relaxation exercises are most effective if practised while lying on the floor, for then the whole body can relax easily, and ten or fifteen minutes should be allowed if the exercise is to be really effective. But unless there's plenty of time, and mats have been brought along with this exercise specifically in mind, the first exercise here may not always be possible during an ordinary group meeting in a hall. With that in mind, other 'loosening up' exercises which can be done while standing or sitting, are also included. However, be careful to pace what you do, especially at first. *Whichever exercise you under-take, never move too quickly and never force your body. If you feel a twinge or an ache, then stop and don't try so hard next time.* Members with a specific medical problem could do the exercise sitting in a chair.

When you relax it is more effective if, instead of just suddenly letting your body flop, you gradually and consciously allow tension to slip away. If you have this muscle control, you can employ it wherever you are without actually having to lie down and you can also target specific muscle areas if necessary. Everyone has his own favourite exercise, but here is a general one to begin with.

Basic relaxation exercise

Find a space. Lie on your back, arms by your side. Stretch out all your body, rather like the points of a star, as if you're trying to reach every point of the room around you. Hold that position for the count of 5 before you allow yourself to return to your former position.

Now close your eyes and start to breathe slowly while you silently talk to your body. See in your mind the top of your head and in thought, tell your scalp and the muscles of your forehead, face and jaw to relax. Take your time. Then slowly relax your neck and shoulders so that you feel as if you're sinking back into a cloud.

Now gradually relax your arms, wrists and hands, pausing each time as you do so, before feeling every other part of your body slowly relax, step by step, until all of you, down to your toes, is relaxed. Continue to breathe gently, letting your mind settle and go quiet – silently repeat a mantra, a word, perhaps, like 'quiet' or 'peace', if it helps.

Rest until you are completely relaxed, physically and mentally. If you do this at home, you could play soft music (and also remember to switch the phone off first!). Lie for a few minutes, concentrating only on your breathing and that warm feeling of peace, before gradually allowing the weight to return to each part of your body in turn, gently stretching your fingers and toes if you feel like it. Rest for a moment, open your eyes and then slowly sit up. Never sit up suddenly – that could make you feel dizzy. Then, when you feel ready, stand up and you're ready for anything!

STANDING EXERCISES

These are designed to free different parts of the body from tension. In each case you should stand comfortably with your feet slightly apart. Repeat each exercise twice:

The whole body

Peepshow

Imagine that you want to see what is happening on the other side of a wall, which is just higher than the top of your head. Put your hands on the top and slowly stretch up on your toes to peer over it. Count 3 as you watch, then somebody turns and you must duck down again. Stand, relax and breathe deeply.

Cleaner

Imagine you are cleaning high windows. You will have to stretch to reach all the corners, but be careful. Now, shake out the cloth and sit in the nearest chair to relax before repeating the exercise, holding the cloth in the other hand.

Colour code

While you are sitting, imagine that you are very cold, think of the colour BLUE. (*pause*).

Now the sun's beginning to shine, things are turning YELLOW, so you can 'unfreeze' a little (*take a breath*).

Now think ORANGE, you're warm now. (*relax a little more*).

Lastly think RED, feel the sun's heat and relax. (*close your eyes and take two deep breaths*).

Remembering the colour code is a quick and easy way of taking your body from tension to a relaxed state – useful as you wait in the wings before going on stage.

Stretch and Melt

Standing, stretch your arms upwards to touch the ceiling. Gradually and smoothly let your arms slowly fall from wrists to shoulders, then down by your sides, as your head drops on to your chest. Allow your spine to melt as your knees relax so that you are standing, drooping forward, your arms hanging loose. Count three, then slowly and carefully straighten your knees and gradually uncurl your spine until your head comes up last and you're standing upright again. Give your body a little shake. Then to loosen your wrists imagine you are shaking water off your hands. To loosen your legs and feet, imagine you have inadvertently walked into a nest of ants – shake them off! Finally, stand tall but with shoulders relaxed and breathe deeply.

HEAD AND NECK AND SHOULDERS

Tension in this part of the body particularly affects speech. To illustrate this, imagine you are standing in a frozen wasteland in just your summer clothes. Now while you are still tensed, say a short poem or a nursery rhyme. Feel how tight your neck and shoulder muscles are – and these are the very muscles which should be relaxed when you speak. What has happened to your voice? It is probably hard and strangled and without much expression. Now stand as if you are warm and happy and completely at ease, and say your verse again. That is how you want to speak, and you do when you're relaxed. An actor must be particularly careful to keep these muscles free at all times and, if necessary, should make sure that they are by loosening them up before going on stage. *Each of the following exercises should be done slowly and only two or three times, with a count of 2 between each movement – and stop if you feel dizzy.*

1. Looking down at the floor, bend your head forward until your chin rests on your chest, return to the normal position, pause, then tilt your head to look at the ceiling, then return to the normal position.
2. Looking ahead, tilt your head to the left ear, straighten up, pause, then tilt towards the right ear, before straightening up again.
3. Turn to look over your left shoulder as far as you can, count three, then return to look forward. Repeat, this time looking over your right shoulder.
4. Shrug your shoulders up and down several times.
5. Stand relaxed, arms by your side. Pull your shoulders as far forward as possible and then pull them back as far as possible, several times.
6. Circle your right arm in a clockwise and then anti clockwise direction. Repeat with the left arm.
7. End by gently shaking loose the upper part of your body, especially your arms and hands – imagine there's sticky paper stuck to your fingers!

For exercises which relax facial muscles, see p167

POSTURE

To maintain a correct posture, it helps to imagine that there is a thread attached to the top of your head which is holding you erect, but it's not so tight as to make your body tense. Your waist is pulled in, your shoulders square, but never tense. Your head is held steady, with your chin level. Your arms hang loosely by your sides, hands with fingers slightly curled so that your thumb nearly touches your forefinger. Know that your weight and energy are centred. You are standing tall but at ease, so that if you had to move in whichever direction, you could do so easily.

When you stand your feet should be slightly apart, your body weight mainly over one foot, with the other resting on the ground to provide support and balance. You will have to shift your body weight, of course (and this is often done unconsciously) but it should be done so smoothly that no-one would notice. Don't sway or shift your feet frequently, especially when you're on stage, and don't let your legs become tense. However, once you know what your correct posture is, you shouldn't consciously think about it too often.

For other notes on posture and characterisation see p177.

16 PERFORMANCE SKILLS 1

what this chapter covers...

In this chapter we consider in some detail the first of two essential aspects of performance skill: the *voice*. Games to help with the understanding and control of breathing, articulation and projection are covered here.

VOCAL PERFORMANCE SKILLS

As we have seen you will never perform well on stage if you are tense, and the relaxed state is just as important for voice production as it is for body movement. Your voice will not have the energy needed to project itself or the feelings it must express unless you are relaxed. So, vocal skills begin with a relaxed state, which is important for expression, projection and clarity, and continue with correct breathing from the diaphragm.

BREATH CONTROL

All of us breathe and speak without even thinking about it, but for the actor correct breathing is paramount to successful voice production. Without this skill you'll be unable to speak clearly or express emotions effectively. You'll run out of breath before you reach the end of a speech, or your voice will drop at the end of a sentence. Here are a few basic exercises to help you breathe correctly. Repeat them two or three times. Find a space and stand relaxed and comfortable with your feet slightly apart.

1. Place your hands at the base of your ribs and as you breathe IN feel the muscles draw the ribs upwards, as your diaphragm descends and your stomach muscles relax. As you breathe OUT the stomach muscles contract, the diaphragm rises and the ribs are drawn down and inwards.

Performance Skills 1 (Vocal)

2 Think of all your muscles as being relaxed. As you breathe IN through your nose, lift your heels, then gently drop back on them (but not so suddenly and hard as to jar the spine) and as you do so, say, '*Ha*'. Repeat this several times and your neck area should feel free. If it doesn't, repeat the neck and shoulder exercises on p162, for not only will you get a sore throat if your neck and throat aren't relaxed, but you'll also strain your voice.

3 Timing the breath. Now breathe IN through your nose to a silent count of 3 as you raise your arms to shoulder height.

As you drop your arms again, gently breathe OUT through your mouth, again to the silent count of 3.

Repeat, only this time, hold the inhaled breath (3) before exhaling. As you improve your breath control you can extend the count number, sometimes varying it so that the number when you breathe in is lower than when breathing out eg breathe in to 4, hold 2, breathe out to 6. Repeat, counting the numbers as you exhale, but don't force your breath, control it.

4 Controlling the breath

a This exercise can be done at home when you have a glass of water and a straw to hand. Having inhaled, blow bubbles into the glass at a controlled rate. Next time, control your breath so that the bubbles flow slowly at first before increasing in speed – and vice versa.

b Here is a sentence introduced in stages (shown by /) as more information is added and more breath control required. Say it first a phrase at a time, gradually adding the next phrase until you can complete the whole sentence with expression but without becoming breathless or dropping your voice.

> 'Now let us go walking on this fine spring morning /
> when the sky is blue and the birds are singing /
> flowers bloom bright in the gardens /
> and all is well in the world around us.'

If your breath control is good, you can pause briefly before a new phrase (for expression) but you should not need to catch another breath until you have finished.

5 Snatching a breath is sometimes necessary in speech. Breathe IN and begin to count aloud, snatching a breath through the mouth again after each 6th number. You will feel your chest expand and realise that using better control of your breath in the first place makes speaking long sentences easier that having to snatch a breath like this.

Emotion and breathing

The way you feel will affect the way you breathe, and as an actor you should be aware of this. As you practise this exercise and express the emotion, notice how your muscles react in order to control your breath. Each time take a short breath.

Say the word '**Yes**' – in *excitement*; as if you're *tired; angry; calm*.

Then '**No**' – in *surprise; angrily*; as if you're *disappointed*; as if you're *tired*; as if you're *frightened*.

Whispering also uses the abdominal muscles to control the breath.

Partners

Stand opposite a partner and speaking in short sentences begin a conversation – start with '*I saw what happened*' or '*Why did you leave?*' When you have both spoken once, take a step away from each other. Repeat this, continuing the conversation, still whispering and never raising your voice. You'll find it requires breath control as well as concentration as you try to convey what you're saying across a large space. You'll also find that you must stay relaxed.

The exercise will become more difficult if you stretch your neck forward in an effort to reach your partner verbally, for you'll tighten the muscles in your neck and throat, your voice will sound strained and you may become breathless.

In groups

With 3 or 4 others, act out a short scene from one of the following, with all conversation carried out in whispers:
- Thieves plan and carry out a robbery;
- You have an argument, but you mustn't wake the baby;
- As soldiers, you move in to surprise the (imagined) enemy;
- You have an argument in a church;
- You arrive home very late, but you mustn't wake your parents.

ARTICULATION

Articulation is the ability to speak clearly and fluently, pronouncing words accurately and distinctly and at a pace which allows the listener to hear and understand what you're saying. To do this you use your lips, jaw, tongue, the roof of your mouth and soft palate. The lips and the jaw, in particular, as well as the tongue, should be flexible so that you can speak clearly. The following exercises are useful as a warm-up before speaking lines, but you should begin by freeing all the facial muscles. The exercises given in this section are only a few of the many that there are.

FACIAL EXERCISES

Facial exercises help mobility both for expression of character and clear speech. These are best done in front of a mirror if one is available – or with a partner if you want some fun! You can do either a) or b), or both.

1. Move your scalp backwards and forwards. Raise your eyebrows, first one and then the other (if you can do it) and then both together. Blink both eyes five times, then wink each eye separately five times. Open your eyes as wide as you can. Wrinkle your nose and using the muscles in your cheeks, try to move it from side to side. Snarl, smile, then yawn.

2. Gently massage your scalp, temples and the sides of your nose, then the back of your neck, the top of your shoulders and your jaw, then yawn. Yawning is a good way of relaxing muscles, especially if you stretch at the same time.

Now move on to the most important parts of the face, which you use when you speak – the lips, jaw and tongue. Say the following without moving either your lips or jaw and you'll see just how important they are – *'Pass Margaret the butter please.'*

VOCAL EXERCISES

Repeat one or two of the following exercises several times and notice how each part of your mouth moves to enable you to speak clearly. Repeat the phrases two or three times, but remember that *precision* is important, not how quickly you can say the words.

The Lips. Purse the lips and move them from side to side.

Press your lips together lightly and blow through them so that they vibrate.

Say the sounds *oo, ee, ow* so that your mouth forms a tube, a wide smile and a circle.

Say the following:

- *bay, bee, buy, boh, boo; pat, pep, pip, pop, pup; fay, fee fie, foe fum; way, wee, why, woe, woo*
- *Peggy Babcock, Peggy Babcock*
- *Fiddle piggy, fiddle piggy, fiddle piggy*
- *Boots and shoes lose newness soon*
- *Popping peas and pink pomegranates*
- *Bobby brought some pretty boots for Baby Bertha*

The Jaw. Drop your jaw, then close your mouth quickly so that you make a popping sound.

Drop your jaw, swing it from side to side, then backwards and forwards.

With your mouth closed, chew a large piece of sticky cake.

Say the following:

- *act, art, ash; odd, out, owl, howl, ow! wow!; va, va, van; quack, quack, quack.*
- *Do sharks bark?*
- *Olly the octopus won an Oscar.*
- *Margaret Clark sat in the park.*
- *Your sock will rot if left on the rock.*
- *Harry hangs his hat on the hanger.*

The Tongue. Put out your tongue and touch the end of your nose, then your chin, your left cheek and your right cheek.

Pretend you're clearing sticky crumbs from behind all your teeth in turn.

Purse your lips and curl your tongue out through them.

With your jaw dropped, flap your tongue quickly behind your teeth.

Say the following, noticing what your tongue is doing:

- *day, dee, dye, doh, do; no, no no; they, thee, thy, then; ray, ree, rye, row roo.*
- *Grey clay held the clue*
- *David dared little Larry twist the twine tighter*
- *Rose limped along the track*
- *I tied my kite to a little tree*

The Soft Palate is the back of the roof of your mouth. It lowers when you make certain sounds, such as *m, n* or *ng*. Say *ah* and slowly change to saying *ng*. Can you feel what's happening? Try saying *long, strong, ring, dancing, performing, humming*.

All together now... Any tongue twister will help you maintain mobility of your mouth and will encourage clear articulation, provided that you remember to say each word clearly rather than trying to say them all quickly. Here are a few to say three times, and you'll know many more:

- *Mrs Smith's fish sauce shop*
- *pack a copper kettle*
- *imagine managing an imaginary menagerie*
- *double bubble gum bubbles double*
- *the slim spider slid slowly sideways*
- *for sheep soup, shoot sheep*
- *freshly fried fresh flesh*
- *three grey geese in a green field grazing*
- *eleven benevolent elephants*
- *red lolly, yellow lorry* (yes, the second word is different from the last!)

Good articulation is especially important to the actor who may have to speak in a dialect, which means you will have to work harder to get that dialect correct. A member of an audience who can not understand what you are saying or who misses dialogue, for whatever reason, soon loses interest.

But an actor does not only need to speak clearly to communicate effectively, he must also speak with feeling and expression.

With this in mind, it is a good idea to read aloud whenever you can – play readings are the perfect opportunity, or perhaps read the bedtime story to a child – you won't get better practice than that. You could also read aloud some of the lyrics from the works of Gilbert and Sullivan – or better still, sing them. Your clarity and articulation will certainly improve if you do.

But remember that when you speak as an actor the expression in your voice will come from an understanding of the character you are playing, and the thoughts and emotion behind the words you are saying.

VOCAL EXPRESSION

When a playwright writes his dialogue, he knows what he wants his characters to communicate, and he hopes that the actors will be able to interpret this through the way in which they deliver the lines. There are six ways of doing this – through pitch, inflection, power, pace, the tone of the voice and through an intelligent use of pauses. If you're in tune with your character in the play you'll probably express yourself well automatically, just as you do every day when you speak. But if you know something about the mechanics behind vocal expression, you'll not only speak with clarity but also with conviction.

PITCH

In ordinary conversation the voice is generally pitched at a medium level, but it may, for some reason (and sometimes subconsciously) change to high or low. As an actor with a script, you must know when this would occur and why, so that by varying pitch you can express yourself more clearly. High and Low pitch can suggest:

- **An emotion**. A high pitch generally indicates a high emotion, excitement, hysteria, incandescent anger; a low pitch could indicate sorrow, tiredness, boredom, secrecy, misery and even menace.

    Using first high and then low pitch, say '*What have you done?*' '*Come over here.*' Can you hear and sense the difference in feeling?

- **A different meaning**. A change of pitch on a single word can change the emphasis in a sentence, changing not only the sense of a character's emotion or intention but also the meaning itself.

    Say each of the following sentences, each time emphasising a different word in turn and you'll notice five totally different meanings:

    'We're going to the theatre on Monday night.'
    'We're going to the theatre on Monday night.'
    'We're going to the theatre on Monday night.'
    'We're going to the theatre on Monday night.'
    'We're going to the theatre on Monday night.

- **Information in parenthesis** – an extra piece of information which could be left out of the sentence without losing the original intention (here giving information about Posey) – for example:

    'Posey, [*who's working in the green house*], is Clay's elder daughter.'

    The pitch of the voice for the phrase in italics should be slightly lower.

Inflection

This is not unlike pitch, for it is a varying of pitch on one word to indicate the sense of what you're saying, the variation being on an upward or downward note.

The final word in a statement generally has a downward inflection – '*I'm going home now.*' Make sure that, as an actor, you don't allow your voice to rise at the end of a statement, because that suggests that the sentence is unfinished, or even that it is a question.

Power

This, too, is closely allied to pitch. It doesn't necessarily mean that your voice grows louder, but more that it grows in strength. This can happen as a climax at the end of a speech, or it can grow gradually during the speech as strength of feeling grows. You will feel this if you read aloud part of a speech from Shakespeare's 'Julius Caesar' when Brutus speaks of him:

> 'As Caesar loved me, I weep for him; as he was fortunate, I rejoice at it; as he was valiant, I honour him; but as he was ambitious, I slew him.'

Pace

When you study a script you will generally find that the pace and rhythm of the lines will be dictated by the writer. He will have worked and reworked them until he has achieved the emotional effect he wants. That is why you should learn scripted words as they are written and not paraphrase them.

Varying the pace, especially in a long speech, will keep the dialogue fresh, interesting and meaningful, but you'll only find the pace at which you should deliver the lines through study of the text.

Tone

The tone of your voice will indicate your mood or emotion, and it will colour the words you're saying. For example, the tone in which you ask the question, '*Will you do it for me?*' will indicate whether you're being demanding or forceful, kind or cajoling, as it will with a simple command like, '*Come here.*'

In everyday life you instinctively vary the pitch, tone and pace of what you say, as you will if you read the simple examples on the next page with a partner.

Scenario 1	Scenario 2
A. Bill Scott's over there.	**B**. Stand still.
B. Bill Scott?	**A**. What?
A. Bill Scott.	**B**. Don't move.
B. Not the Bill Scott.	**A**. Why?
A. Bill Scott, the actor.	**B**. There's a snake.
B. Bill Scott, the actor from 'Dancers'?	**A**. No! Where?
A. 'Skaters.'	**B**. There, by your foot.
B. I'm sure it was 'Dancers'.	**A**. Oh, no!
A. No, 'Skaters.'	**B**. Now, move back slowly.
B. Are you sure?	**A**. I daren't.
A. Yes. He was the one who got married.	**B**. You must – slowly.
B. No, he didn't.	**A**. I'll … one step.
A. Yes, don't you remember?	**B**. Now another.
B. That wasn't Bill Scott.	**A**. Er …I've done it.
A. It was. We'll ask him, OK?	**B**. Now, let's look.
B. Yes, we will. Where is he?	**A**. I daren't.
A. He's over …Oh, he's gone!	**B**. Now … Ah, sorry. It's a stick.

As an actor studying a script, you must understand the character's attitude, thoughts, feelings and intention behind the words before you can hope to say them correctly and convincingly. If you do this you'll say the lines as the playwright meant them to be said without even having to consider which techniques you're using to get it right.

PAUSES

A slight pause can be used rather like vocal punctuation, to help you phrase sentences so that they make sense. (They also remind you to breathe!) In text they are marked as commas (a brief pause) and full stops (slightly longer) and they act as a guide, but you may also need to pause where there is no printed punctuation.

You may need to pause fractionally (/) for a dramatic effect. This may be to give the audience a second to think about what you're going to say – 'The quality of mercy / is not strained,' or have said – 'She is a murderer / you know.'

You may also use a pause to indicate emotion – confusion or anger, tiredness or dejection, for example: 'I'm so tired / I can hardly think.' 'I don't know / what /to do.'

Some playwrights, like Harold Pinter, use the pause to great effect. They are printed as such in the script. They contain a wealth of meaning and unspoken thought, and the actor(s) concerned must convey this in the silence. It is a special skill and as an actor you really have to identify with the character's feelings, and time (feel) the pause exactly, so that you end it before it becomes embarrassing.

Unscripted pause. There is one other occasion when you should pause, but it will never be scripted and will generally only happen during a comedy. This is when you hold your line rather than speak it, because the audience is laughing at a previous line or piece of action. You must always pause long enough for the audience to enjoy their laughter, don't speak through it. If you do, your lines won't be heard, the point of your saying them will be missed and the audience will feel cheated because they weren't allowed time to enjoy a funny moment. With practice, you'll 'feel' when you should pick up the dialogue again. Just be aware that next time the laugh might not come in the same place. Every audience is different

PROJECTION

Projection is the very necessary art of reaching every member of the audience vocally, and it is one thing which every new actor worries about. One thing you must not do is strain physically to 'throw' your voice to the back of the room. Good projection comes, above all, from **preparation, concentration, intention and confidence**.

PREPARATION

You prepare yourself **mentally**, over a period of time, by studying the lines and knowing what you are going to say. Through rehearsal, you'll also know how you're going to say them, because, hopefully, you will have become your character. You must concentrate on this during rehearsal and again once you're on stage.

Before the show, you prepare yourself **physically** by breathing deeply, relaxing your neck, throat and upper body and by warming up your voice in the dressing room – sing up and down the scales perhaps. It helps if you can lubricate your throat by drinking some water before you go on stage – water, not milk. As any trained singer will tell you, milk has the effect of increasing any mucus in the throat, so restricting the work of the larynx and vocal chords. In the wings, you consciously relax yourself and prepare to switch on your energy the minute you go on stage. Once there, make sure that you breathe from the diaphragm and keep concentrating.

INTENTION

Your intention is to share your character and his part in the play with your audience, and you intend to do this well. When you speak you are not just going to try to reach the audience, you are going to *include* them — even the little old lady sitting in the back row. After all, they have taken the trouble to come and support you. You must keep in mind that you intend your voice to reach whichever part of the hall you decide on, and know that you will succeed without having to shout.

CONFIDENCE

These preparations will bring with them the confidence you need to project your voice. Remind yourself that because of all that preparation you have done, everyone will hear what you say because *you know what you are doing, and what you are going to say is worth hearing.* So take a deep breath and believe in yourself. Switch on the energy in your voice on the very first word. That says 'I have confidence in myself,' and if the audience believes that, they'll relax and listen. No-one in that hall wants you to fail, and many of them know that they would never have the courage to do what you're about to do — act on a stage. Stop worrying, go for it and your own confidence will carry your voice to the back of the hall with ease.

This advice also applies to any public speaking. As long as you are organised, well prepared and know your subject well, the confidence that knowledge brings will enable you to speak clearly and with conviction, whatever the subject.

17 PERFORMANCE SKILLS 2

what this chapter covers...

The second half of our discussion of performance skills deals with physical performance, and in this chapter we will consider how to create characters through posture, movement and gesture and how body language can drastically affect the meaning of the words in the script.

PHYSICAL PERFORMANCE SKILLS

There are many aspects to performing, and although, having read the script, you may know what the play is about, the script itself is not the whole story. The playwright has created the plot, the characters and the dialogue, but it is the actor, with his director, who brings it all to life. So how do you do that?

BODY LANGUAGE

Speech is the most obvious means of communication, but although we may not realise it, body language is equally important. Body language means movements made by the body, generally involuntary, which give obvious or subliminal signals, clues to our intention/motivation, and our reaction to any emotion, person or situation. Millions of years ago, before language as we know it came into being, man's thoughts and feelings were expressed through noises, movement and gesture. Early research carried out in the 1950s by Albert Mehrabian, a researcher in body language, showed that in most cases today communication is still, on average, 45% verbal and 55% non-verbal. So it is not only how you say things, but also what your body is indicating when you say them, for body language is closely linked to thought and feeling. That's why telephone calls and emails are not as satisfactory as speaking to someone face to face, for you're not able to gauge their non-verbal reaction to what you're saying.

Our bodies react to a pattern of '**thought → emotion → action**' and that action is a conscious or unconscious movement of some kind. For example, when you feel nervous, you may bite your lip; when you're happy, you smile; your brow furrows when you're worried or angry. You give these signals without even thinking about it. Here's a quick experiment which may prove the point (answers are at the foot of the page):

1. Think of a picture you've seen, remember the detail. Now, while you were thinking, where did you look?
2. Now think of a tune that you know, hear it in your head. Where did you look this time?
3. Try to recall an emotion, a time when you had very strong, personal feelings about something. Think about it. Where did you look?
4. Finally, when you're told to begin, talk to yourself, just start a little monologue, until you're told to stop. It doesn't matter what you say, because everybody else will be talking too.

So parts of your body, in this case your eyes, move even when you're not aware of it.

EYE CONTACT

While on the subject of eye movement, do remember that eye contact is an important and vital way of reading another person's intention, attitude and even to some extent, their thoughts. As an actor you should, where possible, maintain eye contact when you speak directly to someone on stage. There is nothing worse than talking to someone who looks at your forehead or over the top of your head when he addresses you. Try this group exercise which will illustrate the importance of eye contact in relation to emotion as well as communication.

TESTING EYE CONTACT

Everyone stands in a space and then:

1. Walk round the room, but as you do so, don't look at anyone, avoid their gaze and make a mental note of how you feel.

Answers to experiment above

1. *The chances are that you looked up to your left.*
2. *You probably looked either to your right or left with your head slightly tilted.*
3. *Most people look down to their right.*
4. *Did you look down left towards the floor? Many people do.*

2 Now walk round again, but this time look at everyone you pass. How do you feel this time – probably happier and part of the group again. It's unlikely that you'll feel as isolated and alone as you did when you avoided eye contact.

FACIAL EXPRESSION

Facial expressions are also a guide to thought and emotion and we often consciously change these to hide what we're actually feeling – as when talking to small children in a worrying situation.

It goes without saying, therefore, that when you're in a play, your body language will go a long way toward helping you bring your new character to life, but you must know what the character's thoughts and emotions are, so that your body has the motivation it needs to respond in the correct way.

CREATING CHARACTER PHYSICALLY

Try now to create a new 'you' physically.

POSTURE

When you are acting, your own natural posture may need to change. Stand in a space as yourself and then decide on your new 'you'. Will you stand tall and upright, or craven and hollow-chested? What is your status in life, for status is also something which could affect your body language. Where is your centre of energy? Do you 'lead' with your chin so that you look down on everyone, or do you stick out your stomach and swagger? Remember the animals? (p148). What kind of animal might characterise you? Are you a serious, wise owl, still but watchful for most of the time, or a heavy hippo? Are you light on your feet or do you walk with a heavy tread, for even the way you walk gives an indication of character as well as age, mood and motivation. But do try to be accurate in your movements – you only have to ask a six-year old to walk like an old person to see how misinformed some interpretations can be!

WALKING

The following exercises show how thought and intention/motivation affect your posture and the way you move. Find a space and when told to, move across the room in character after pausing to consider what your thoughts are when you're told that:

1. You are shy but you have to enter a room full of strangers at a party.
2. On the way home from shopping it begins to rain heavily, but you have no umbrella.
3. You are old and you must pass a group of rowdy teenagers on the pavement.
4. You arrive home having just won a medal at the Olympics.
5. On a holiday beach you're the only one who isn't sun-tanned.
6. You have had too much to drink, but you don't want anyone to know.

The way you moved probably changed when you heard the instruction, which in turn altered your thoughts and intention.

Conversely your body language can affect how you feel:

Stand at ease in a space, and as yourself, imagine that your source of energy is in your chest. Now that you are conscious of it, let that energy give you the power to walk round the room, wherever you want to. You will be walking tall as you normally do.

1. Now, mince around as if you are very prim and proper. Has this affected the way the rest of your body moves and what you're feeling or thinking?
2. Walk now with a loping action. Did you find that your thoughts changed as well as your posture?
3. Move with the weight on your heels as you take each step. How did you feel? Did your character change? What sort of person did you imagine you might be?

Gesture

As the new character you are creating, are you the sort of person who stands, arms folded in a defensive position, or an expansive man who sticks his thumbs in his braces? Do you show nervousness by shifting from one foot to the other? We use gesture in many ways, sometimes

- To express emotion (holding hands up to the face in shock or raising a fist in anger).
- In conventional ways (shaking hands in greeting or waving goodbye).
- As an expression of an inner emotion which we may even be trying

to hide (wringing hands in anxiety, twitching or drumming fingers impatiently). These can be useful to an actor when used in character, as long as they're not over-used or too repetitive. No audience likes to watch an actor who doesn't seem able to speak without using his hands.

But even gestures themselves can alter your body movement as your intention strengthens or changes. To illustrate:

Imagine your friend is standing a short distance away and beckon him to come to you in the following ways (in each case he will not respond) a) hesitantly; b) as an ordinary demand; c) be a little more determined; d) angrily.

Did your body change – tense perhaps – as your intention to make him obey increased?

ENTRANCES AND EXITS

To sustain characterisation, you should know your motivation and how you're feeling before you make an entrance or leave the stage. Don't enter and then suddenly remember why you're there. Try moving correctly as you say the following phrases. If you work as a group of four, you could each take a different adverb while using the same phrase and the others can tell you if you're convincing.

Enter an imaginary room saying:

- *'I'm here.'* a) happily; b) reluctantly; c) fearfully; d) in exasperation.

- *'Where is he?'* a) excitedly; b) angrily; c) anxiously; d) tearfully.

- *'I've something to say.'* a) as a matter of fact; b) angrily; c) happily; d) as a confession;

Exits. In a group as before, each speaker begins by sitting, pausing for a second and then leaving after saying:

- *'I'll go.'* a) in exasperation; b) lazily; c) in anticipation; d) angrily.

- *'I'll phone tomorrow.'* a) happily; b) sleepily; c) angrily; d) tearfully.

- *'Goodnight.'* a) sleepily; b) tearfully; c) angrily; d) lovingly.

Sitting

Remember that not only the nature of your character, but also the period in which the play is set will dictate how you sit. Men and women each sit in a different way – men generally with knees apart, women feet together or legs crossed. Victorian ladies did not sit with legs crossed. New actors sometimes even find the very act of sitting difficult. Unless you actually move across to the seat immediately before you sit, you may find yourself shuffling backwards or sideways if you're not aware of just how near you are to the edge of the chair. So, if you know you have to sit, during rehearsal you should note where the chair is and align yourself near to it, and when standing in front of it just feel the edge of the seat behind your legs. Note, too, on the dress rehearsal, just how high or low it is. If it's a very low chair, you may have to sit on the edge or very upright if you're not to feel inferior to another whose seat is higher. Whether you lower yourself gently into a chair, or flop will depend on your character!

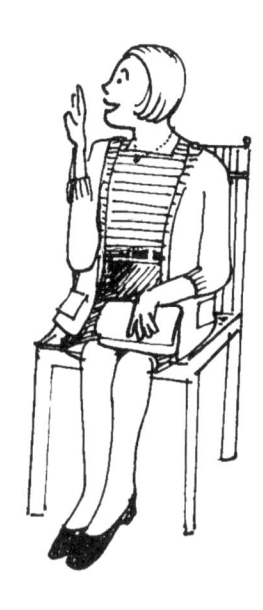

Energy

This is something every actor needs and should display from his very first entrance. It is an almost indefinable quality, and it doesn't mean that you burst on to the stage like a madman or say your lines with great power. Rather, your energy lights you from within, making the audience want to watch you. It will show in your voice as a certainty, which comes from really knowing your character and your lines. Just as someone will smile if you smile at him, so if you show through this 'energy' that you are in control, the audience will believe in you, sit back and know they're in safe hands. They feel what you feel, so don't show your nervousness or embarrassment on stage! Notice the times at the beginning of a rehearsal when a lack of energy is quite obvious. Actors droop on the stage and say the lines as if they're bored or tired, even though they're not. But if you pretend that was just a warm-up and begin again, this time remembering to 'switch on' your life, the scene will take on life as well and it will be interesting to watch.

Most of the activities in the following chapters on Improvisation and Mime will help you practise many different ways of expressing character through body language. But before you proceed to this, we should perhaps consider the links between memory and imagination.

MEMORY AND IMAGINATION

Memory and imagination are often so inextricably linked in the mind that it can be difficult for an actor to analyse which of these helped in his recreation of a scene or a character. But occasionally it is interesting to analyse which of these two attributes are the stronger in one's makeup. Both can be made stronger with practice. The following exercise can involve either or both, depending on the individual.

MIND WALK

Members sit and follow instructions, painting pictures in their minds without physically moving. The instructions should be given quietly and slowly, allowing members time to create in their minds the journey they're making.

'You're going on an imaginary journey in your mind, just a walk, but you'll remember the details of it, so close your eyes and relax.

Before you set off, look round and see where you are, feel the ground beneath your feet, know how you're feeling

(*pause*)

Now, you're walking along a public highway, notice what it's like, see what's on either side of you, notice the air, the atmosphere, the people if there are any. As you walk on, notice the sky, what it's like.

(*pause*)

The area around you is changing a little now, the road narrows, but you don't mind that, you keep walking. You can see some buildings in the distance. You walk towards them and you find that there's one in particular which interests you more than the others. You walk towards it and then you just stand at look at it.

(*pause*)

Look at the detail there – the walls, the windows, the colours, the surroundings, all the other things you can see. You see a door. Look at it. What's it like? Notice the detail.

Then you see that it's partly open. Oh, you must just go and look inside before you go back home. So you walk up to the door and give it a slight push. It opens wider, so you peep inside and you see … Now hold that vision, remember it.

(*pause*)

Now, I want you to take a deep breath, then slowly open your eyes.

(*pause*)

Now, tell us about your walk.'

The results, when the 'walks' are recounted, always prove to be varied and interesting and in some the detail is very precise. Analysis by each member can give an insight into whether what he 'saw' was pure imagination, accurate recall of a factual event, or a mixture of both. There can be a wide variation among members, but it may serve to remind players that when they act, they can use both of these skills to advantage.

18 CREATIVE DRAMA

what this chapter covers…

With group members now relaxed, concentrating and aware of the fundamentals of acting, it is time to get creative! In this chapter we will look at the value of spontaneity and mime in creating engaging drama from very simple ideas.

IMPROVISATION AND MIME

A leader suggesting any form of improvisation or mime may be met by groans and shudders from members who shrink into themselves and exclaim, 'Oh, no. I can't do that!' And maybe even the leader, if he has never tried it for himself, won't realise just how valuable an activity it can be, for it enriches the drama experience and can be most enjoyable. It frees the mind, and confidence grows along with imagination.

If you think about it, many people improvise in a small way every day, without ever realising that's what they are doing. Have you never made up a convincing reason (excuse) when you've been late for an appointment or done something which you shouldn't have done; or improvised a movement by suddenly bending to tie a shoelace (even though you may be wearing slip-ons) when you don't want someone to notice you? Young children improvise all the time. Listen to them play in a Wendy House or round a dressing up box, or watch them use a cardboard box in so many different ways.

IMPROVISATION

Improvisation in its simplest form is acting spontaneously, using memory recall and your imagination, everyday language and physical movement – and making it up as you go along. That's all it is. But in a drama group situation it's great fun and a valuable activity. It brings to those who practise it more understanding of life and of themselves, and through this, a confidence which allows the nervous to try something new, the reticent to become more outgoing and it even, perhaps, makes the intolerant more tolerant. It also has the advantage of being new and original, unique even, every time it's undertaken. Improvisation

- Allows participants to explore characters other than their own and situations they may never have been in, or ever will be.

- Increases the ability to understand emotions, both your own and those of others, and provides an opportunity to express them, as well as thoughts and ideas, in an articulate way. If an actor becomes practised in doing this using his own words, he'll bring this ability into any study of a script written by someone else.

- Encourages spontaneity, so improving language skills and the ability to respond quickly in an appropriate and coherent manner.

- Encourages interaction with others, improving the ability to share and co-operate and exchange ideas – something everyone needs, especially on the stage.

- Develops the imagination, which is a particularly useful skill in acting, and encourages creativity.

- Used in conjunction with a play which is in rehearsal, it may enable both the producer and the player to come to a deeper understanding of a character, a scene or even of the dialogue itself (see p113).

When using Improvisation, you as the leader should

- Always make sure that the work attempted is introduced and carried out in a friendly, cooperative, caring way. The group is, after all, a socially based group, and nobody should be made to do what they don't want to do. If you could start the ball rolling by taking part yourself, your enthusiasm should encourage all members to join in the fun.

- Know what you hope members will achieve from any activity and how you may be able to help them carry it forward.

- Start with simple ideas, varying the type of exercise as time progresses, and be prepared to carry over any which promises to grow into an 'event' – such as a duologue or group work which needs more time to perfect. It might even become a sketch or short

Creative Drama

play – although this may not have been the aim of the exercise.

- Be sure to give instructions clearly and precisely before the activity begins, making sure that members understand exactly what they're to do before you give them the signal to begin.
- Know the approximate time you want to give to that particular exercise.
- Move round, noting work which is good and which may serve as an example, helping where members may appear to be in difficulty.
- Be prepared to stop the exercise if it's foundering.
- Warn when it's nearly time to end, before finally giving a clear instruction to stop.
- Allow time for members to show what they've done, bearing in mind that there may not be enough time for everyone to do so. At first, the 'showing' should take place in the area where it was practised, but as members become more aware of positioning in relation to their audience, a 'stage space' could be adopted at one end of the room where all partner or group improvisation is shown.

It will make your work much easier if you transfer some of the activities, especially those with multiple ideas, into card format, as has sometimes been illustrated here. It takes time, but once done they are ready for use whenever needed and this format will save time in future explanation and organisation. It also means that members could use them in the event of the organiser being absent or busy elsewhere. Naturally you will also add many of your own ideas to those given, as well as instigating other original activities.

MIME

This art form is the perfect example of the specific use of body language to convey ideas and thought. Through it you can tell stories, express thoughts, feelings and intention so well that anyone watching knows exactly what is happening and no words are necessary. Some of the exercises already used employ mime to some degree, but in this chapter we look specifically at mime and see how its skills link to the actor's craft. The first activities are mime in its simplest form.

Individual mime

Everyone joins in and stands near a chair. Following your instructions, they will mime the following:

Tea-time

You're standing in the kitchen and you're going to make a cup of tea and then, when it's ready, sit down and drink it. Begin. Watch, and when they've finished ask if anyone forgot any detail, such as switching on the kettle in the first place!

Post!

Everyone sits. They're waiting for a postal delivery. On your signal, they go to the door to pick up/receive the post before returning to the chair to open it. They must show by their reaction what this item of post contained and the effect it has on them.

1. A letter has just dropped through your letterbox. Go and get it!
2. Here's the postman. He's brought you a very heavy parcel.

If it's a parcel, did they remember to open and close the door when collecting it? Did the 'parcel' appear to be heavy?

Supermarket

(If the group is large, work no more than ten at a time. A small table should be placed at one end of the room to represent the check-out – it could have a member of staff there or be a self service check-out.) Imagine you're doing the weekly shopping. Take your trolley or basket and move round, taking no more than eight goods from the shelves, moving in such a way as to show what they are. You ask for help if necessary – but remember that this is mime and you may not speak! Sit down at the end to show you're home. Discuss how effective the mimes were.

'Shore' thing

Everyone sits along the longest side of the room, facing across to a part of the 'beach' which will be their own space. Then you give the instruction:

> At last you have five minutes to go down to the beach and you're determined to enjoy yourself. How will you spend that short time, paddling, playing in the sand, beach- combing, gazing out to sea? You decide. Now go and have fun!

Creative Drama

After a few minutes call members back to their seats and discuss what they did.

REWIND

Having completed any of the last mimes, players might then rewind them, as you rewind a video-tape. It would be best to begin this exercise by repeating the chosen mime first – probably the simplest one. Trying to remember a sequence of moves backwards needs a great deal of concentration and should be done slowly. This forms a useful introduction to some of the group mimes later.

COLLECTIVE MIME

MIME CIRCLE

(This can be done while the group is sitting).

Mime circle involves physical expressions of feelings and movement, which arise out of true memory, imagination or, more often, imagination coloured by some true or mistaken information.

The group, sitting in a circle, is told that they are going to mime passing an object from one to the other round the circle. They must indicate what the object is through movement and expression, and others must judge how accurate their mimes are. You, as leader will tell them what the object is, but this will change as it is slowly passed from hand to hand. The change-over should be done slowly and deliberately so that both the action and reaction are clearly seen when one thing changes to another.

For example, the object could start off as '*a heavy parcel ... now it's a baby rabbit ... it's changed to a sticky sweet*'. It is best if the leader has already listed the objects he'll mention so that there's no break in the flow. The list is limited only by the leader's imagination, but here are a few ideas to get you started:

wet pondweed	a worm	hedgehog	baby rabbit
full cup of tea	heavy box	pin	kitten
diamond ring	ticking bomb	a butterfly	a squishy cake
perfumed flower	a bowl of soup	a beetle	a bouquet
perfumed sachet	bird in a cage	smelly socks	a snake

The Walk

Members move round the room, listening to your voice and reacting appropriately. This is best used after a warm up when members move to stand in a space, or if sitting, they are told to put on (imaginary) light sandals, for they're going for a walk. Remember to watch the participants, describe what you 'see' vividly and time the instructions so that they have time to see/feel what you describe and have time to do what you say.

'Now, off you go. It's a lovely sunny day and you're strolling along a country lane – see those pretty flowers, hear the birds – there's a field gate, open it and walk along that path beside the corn – it's rather narrow but you'll manage. Oh no, the ground's rather wet here – and there's a large puddle.

(*pause while they negotiate it*)

Now the path is very stony, can you feel the sharp stones? – but carry on – look to your right, there's an orchard, don't the apples look good? You're hungry now – there's nobody around; why don't you pick one – have you room for another in your pocket? Take a few, but then perhaps you'd better move on, someone might come.

(*pause*)

Oh no, the only way out is through the hedge – look, there's a small hole – can you get through? – oh, it's hard

(*pause*)

but yes, you'll just make it – your sandal, it's got caught – rescue it.

(*pause*)

Oh no! There's someone coming – hurry! Get out of this field – come on, hurry! – you've come to a stream – you'll have to cross it, but there's no bridge.

(*pause*)

Look – stepping stones, you'll have to use those – careful (*pause*)

Fig 17. Picking and storing apples.

Go on, you'll just make it – one final jump – there! You're on firm ground again. It's beginning to rain now – which way is home? stand and make sure – yes, it's that way – hurry, there's a storm brewing – quickly – hurry – have you got the apples? – keep going – there's your garden – up the path – through the door – phew, you're home at last! Find a chair, sit and take off those wet sandals! (*pause*) What an adventure!

There are many variations of this – through mud and over gates, exploring a ruin or trying to hitch a lift, tiptoeing through rows of plants or over a ploughed field, crossing a rickety bridge or ending up in quicksand! It is suggested that you only use the last idea when members are physically fit, know each other well and the hall floor is clean! The only limitations will be in the leader's mind, but plan the route and pitfalls first, know where you're going and don't put your members in any situation where they may really get hurt!

PARTNER AND GROUP MIMES

The following mimes are short but form a good introduction to the longer activities suggested later.

ACTION!

The group is divided into two equal lines **A** and **B**, standing about two metres away from each other. Using only gesture and facial expression, a member from each line in turn (**A** then **B**) should mime doing something in detail and their partner, having guessed what it is, must repeat every movement. Ideas include:

> cutting a lemon in half and eating it;   enjoying a bar of chocolate;
>
> chopping an onion;   seeing a wasp buzzing nearby;   removing a sock;
>
> angrily telling the partner to leave;   beckoning him to come;
>
> mixing and frying a pancake;   making chips;   opening champagne;
>
> polishing an item of silver;   cleaning shoes;   crocheting;
>
> stitching embroidery;   plaiting an imaginary child's hair;
>
> arranging flowers in a vase;   resetting a stopped clock.

The more complicated the mime, the better, but all the detail must be observed for it to be repeated correctly.

(The obvious extensions to this are the 'What's my Line?' game or Charades.)

Rhymes and Stories

The following lend themselves to mime. The topics are given out to the relevant number of members needed, who work and then 'show' to the others who must guess the rhyme or story. The number of participants is shown in brackets. (It is easier for the organiser if the topics are on cards, a sample of which is shown below.)

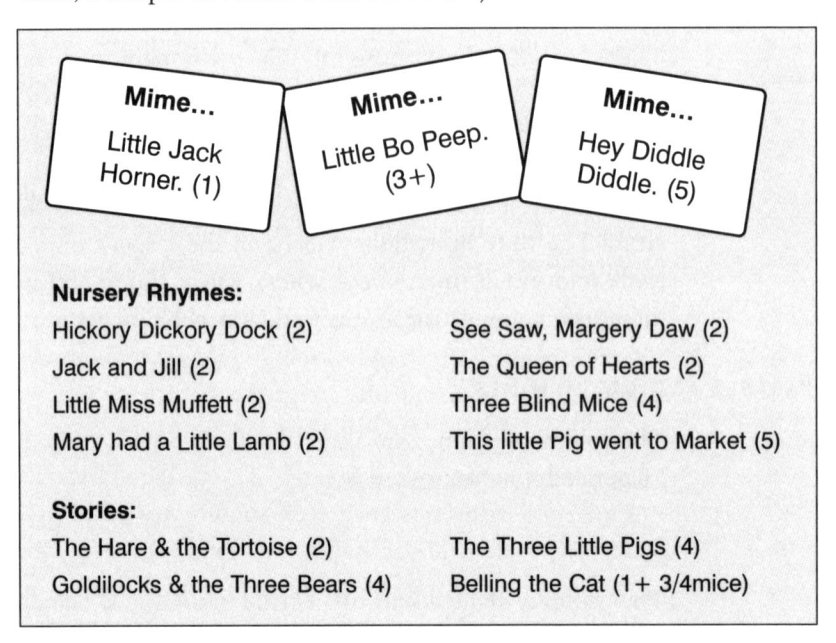

> Mime... Little Jack Horner. (1)
>
> Mime... Little Bo Peep. (3+)
>
> Mime... Hey Diddle Diddle. (5)

Nursery Rhymes:

Hickory Dickory Dock (2)	See Saw, Margery Daw (2)
Jack and Jill (2)	The Queen of Hearts (2)
Little Miss Muffett (2)	Three Blind Mice (4)
Mary had a Little Lamb (2)	This little Pig went to Market (5)

Stories:

The Hare & the Tortoise (2)	The Three Little Pigs (4)
Goldilocks & the Three Bears (4)	Belling the Cat (1 + 3/4 mice)

Mini-scenes for groups of 3-6

Each of the following should be mimed, although a short discussion is allowed first for the participants to draft out the story, which should be kept short and to the point. The actions should be detailed and clear, showing through mime only, action and reaction. It is best if little choice of title is given from the following:

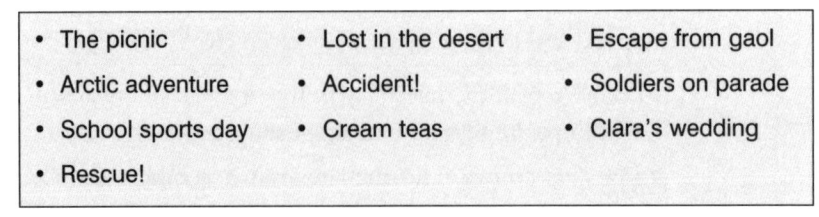

- The picnic
- Arctic adventure
- School sports day
- Rescue!
- Lost in the desert
- Accident!
- Cream teas
- Escape from gaol
- Soldiers on parade
- Clara's wedding

Commentary

Only one in the group may speak, the others mime the action which will be commentated on (where no 'end' is obvious, one should be devised):

Creative Drama

- The Fashion Parade
- Jane visits the Doctor
- Defusing a Bomb
- Victorian Laundry Day
- Egg & spoon Race
- The Boys hang a Picture
- A Visit to the Hairdresser
- Boat Race
- Pitching Tent
- Disco Time

Silent Movies

These activities are great fun and they encourage all the acting skills, especially concentration. It is an opportunity for players to over-act, to use melodramatic movement and extravagant gesture to portray emotion. Ideally, the group should be of no more than 3 or 4 and each character should be clearly defined. The instruction should be to 'keep it simple', for both timing and co-ordination between the actors is essential.

Allow five minutes for 'casting' and storyline discussion before mime rehearsal begins. The movie itself should take no more than 4 or 5 minutes. Use only one title or give a choice of two or three. After rehearsal, the groups show their movie.

1. Begin by acting out the story as a straight-forward silent movie. Only when this has been seen should you build in 2 and then 3 (below) – then players will understand why everything had to be simple! For example, the dumb waiter might do no more than give each customer the wrong plate and then have to return to change the order – not so easily done backwards! Choose from one of the following:

   - The Dumb Waiter
   - The Pipe of Peace.
   - Tramp in Love
   - The Tea Dance.
   - Shoot-out
   - A Bar in the Wild West
   - The Intruder
   - The Stripper
   - Stop Thief!
   - The Proposal

2. Now repeat the movie, with the first half of the action being in slow motion, the second half at speed.

3. Play the movie and then rewind it – best if the exercise 'rewind' (p187) has been used during a previous session.

19 IMPROVISED DRAMA

what this chapter covers...

In this final chapter, we draw together all the skills learned in this section of the book. Here participants are given starting points for a huge variety of drama improvisations which will test what they have learned and help them to develop even further.

IMPROVISED DRAMA

This section is a logical progression from mime and many, in fact, find the activities easier to do because they can speak! Now that dialogue comes into play, the scope for drama widens considerably. Players have more freedom to experiment and the resulting scenes have an added depth of thought and emotion, as well as more interplay of relationships – not only in the scene but between the participants themselves. The examples given have all been found to work and if presented as cards (such as those illustrated), can be used over a period of time.

INDIVIDUAL ACTIVITIES

The following ideas encourage spontaneity and confidence because everyone works at once, and each knows that he's less likely to be noticed or his voice heard. The result may be noisy, but as leader, you can monitor what's happening and occasionally stop the group, to watch or listen to someone who is willing to show his work.

CONVERSATIONS

Everyone finds a space and imagines that they have a mobile phone in their pockets. On the signal, each 'answers' his phone and carries on a conversation. We only hear one side, of course, but his words and attitude should be so convincing that the listener can guess what the conversation's about – which is what members do when they're asked to stop to watch someone continue his phone call.

Soap Box

Everyone has their own favourite topic about which they have very firm views, whether anyone else agrees or not.

1 At a signal everyone addresses the room as if he were on his soapbox, while at the same time listening for the Leader's instruction to stop. Then in turn, one or two can continue, speaking to members of the group who will actually be listening to him!

2 This time the 'speakers' should use a controlling emotion as they 'lecture'. It may be love, hate, envy, anger, fear – whatever they choose – and the topic can be serious or frivolous. Again, choose those who wish to share their thoughts. (You may allow 'heckling' if you judge that the speaker can handle it, but that may be better left until the group has consolidated and the players are more confident.)

Focus

Each member stands in a space facing his chair, but a short distance away from it. He must then imagine that it is whatever he is told it is, but he has to pass it, deal with it or use it. He must show that he believes it's real, by using appropriate body language and speech. The leader then suggests to the group one of the following. It may be:

- a snake on a rock
- a fierce dog
- a bird in a cage
- a large heavy sealed box
- a throne.
- an abandoned baby in a pram
- a shopping bag left on a path
- a deaf man asleep in a wheelchair
- a tiger before the open door of its cage
- an abandoned car with its engine running

PARTNERS

Improvisation is most satisfactory if it's created with a partner or as a member of a group, for it gives the opportunity for shared involvement and interaction. The ideas in the first 'vocal' section result in a conversation, often confrontational, but without a great deal of action, (which is what, at this stage, they are designed to do) and it's wisest only to use one or two at a time, perhaps after a physical warm up. In each case the participants are **A** and **B** who should take it in turns to lead the scene. Partnerships should change frequently.

With a partner – Vocal

Questions, questions!

A and **B** hold a conversation using only a) questions or b) just one or two words until one fails to reply correctly. They are timed and the winning partnership is that which can converse longest without a mistake.

Pardon?

A and **B** hold a conversation, but speak only in gibberish (unintelligible speech) or sounds. This gives players practice in expressing themselves using only inflection, tone of voice and pace.

One line Duologue

An exercise in spontaneity where a single line starts a conversation. There should be no previous discussion and the organiser decides whether it is **A** or **B** who says the line. Here are some ideas to start with:

'Look at the mud on your shoes!'	'What are you doing here?
'I've got a message for you.'	'I'm sorry about last night.'
'What a waste of money.'	'Why didn't you tell me?'
'Where have you been?'	'Call yourself a friend'
'I wasn't expecting you.'	'I've changed my mind.'
'What's the matter?'	'I'm going out.'
'You look awful!'	'Hey look over there.'
'Must you do that now?'	'You read my diary?'
'Don't be such a misery.'	'Stop picking on me.'
'I'm fed up with you.'	'Why is it always my fault?

Character duologue

This time each participant takes on a character, preferably one who has some relationship with the other. When they have decided on their characters, the duologue begins with two lines:

A. I'm just going out.	**B**. Do you have to?
A. Come over here.	**B** No.
A. That looks nice.	**B**. I've just bought it.
A. Look at that!	**B** It's mine.
A What are you doing?	**B** Mind your own business.
A I've lost my job.	**B** What did you do?

A I'm telling my mum.

A Leave me alone!

A Don't, it's dangerous!

A. I don't want to go.

B I don't care

B. But you've got to listen.

B. Who says?

B. But you must!

SITUATION DUOLOGUE

In every case **A** and **B** must bear in mind what he really believes, wants (his intention), or has to do, and he may need to change the approach in his argument in order to try to achieve this. There should be no discussion before the duologue begins and it doesn't matter who speaks first.

A short scene takes place in a:

Shop	**A** intends to buy an item of clothing. **B** tries to persuade him/her otherwise.
Hospital	**A** visits a sleepy, long lost friend. **B** doesn't remember who it is.
Surgery	**A** anxiously visits the doctor. **B**, as the doctor, diagnoses and advises.
Hairdresser's	**A** wants the usual haircut. **B** wants him/her to try the latest style.
Waiting Room	**A** wants to join the armed forces. **B** is against the idea.
Street	**A** wants to see a murder film. **B** prefers a comedy at another cinema.
Office	**A** is trying to finish some work. **B** wants to gossip.
Aeroplane	**A**, about to do a parachute jump, refuses. **B** has to persuade him to do it.
Tent	**A** awakes and hearing a noise wants to leave. **B** refuses.
Gym	**A** is using some equipment. **B** insists he/she is using it incorrectly.
Shared bedroom	**A** is always untidy. **B** likes everything neat.
Bank	There's a robbery. **A** wants to fight back. **B** wants to run.

Character driven duologues

These activities focus on the movement and body language of character and the motivation behind it, as well as the necessary language skills. Members work in twos as before, **A** and **B**, and they are told their characters. Then the location of a scene is given – each couple could have the same location or choice of another might be given. Either **A** or **B** may start the conversation, but they must stay in character.

	CONFRONTATION	
Scene	**A**	**B**
A party	is pompous and conceited	is nervous and shy
A Pub	just wants a quiet drink	is drunk
School Reunion	has just left school	is a very old ex-pupil
On board ship	is going on holiday	is an escaped prisoner
Hospital ward	is a frightened patient	is a pessimistic visitor
Library	is stiff and serious librarian	is very deaf
Expensive Wine Bar	is rich but dirty	is a well-mannered waiter
Disco	loves the loud music	hates everything about it
Art Gallery	is intent on stealing a picture	is security Guard
Bedroom	just out of the bath finds	who is a burglar

Moods

In this exercise body language sets the mood, for what happens between **A** and **B** is suggested by the way they stand or sit and there is no rule as to who starts the conversation. Each member takes a card (unseen) from the pack (illustrated opposite) and, without conferring, takes the position which is suggested there. The physical attitude they take should suggest to each a mood or an intention, and each should decide in his own mind – without conferring – what that may be, and he should know why he feels like that. Both the reply to the first line

Improvised Drama

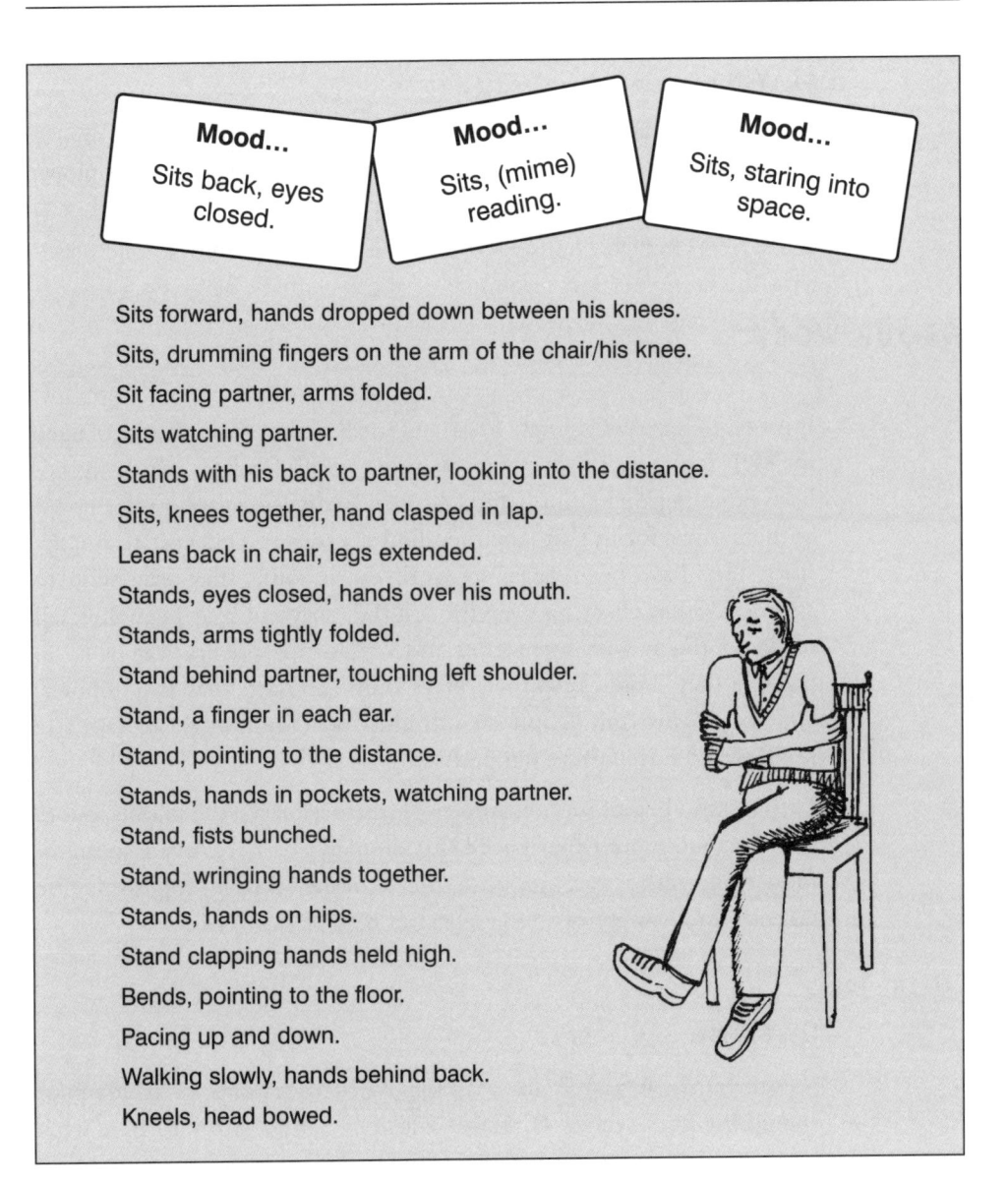

Mood... Sits back, eyes closed.

Mood... Sits, (mime) reading.

Mood... Sits, staring into space.

Sits forward, hands dropped down between his knees.
Sits, drumming fingers on the arm of the chair/his knee.
Sit facing partner, arms folded.
Sits watching partner.
Stands with his back to partner, looking into the distance.
Sits, knees together, hand clasped in lap.
Leans back in chair, legs extended.
Stands, eyes closed, hands over his mouth.
Stands, arms tightly folded.
Stand behind partner, touching left shoulder.
Stand, a finger in each ear.
Stand, pointing to the distance.
Stands, hands in pockets, watching partner.
Stand, fists bunched.
Stand, wringing hands together.
Stands, hands on hips.
Stand clapping hands held high.
Bends, pointing to the floor.
Pacing up and down.
Walking slowly, hands behind back.
Kneels, head bowed.

and to what follows should be logical. The action must begin with a pause, which is broken by either **A** or **B**.

'I SAID ...'

This activity adds further variety to this type of work, and extends the imagination. Either **A** or **B** assumes the position on a card from the 'Moods' pack (above) while his partner starts the duologue by using a random line given to him by the organiser from the list given from One line Duologue on p194.

Leaving

Players **A** and **B** should assume a character with some relationship to the other – parent & child; brother & sister; husband & wife; employer & employee; teacher & pupil; pop star & manager; dance teacher & pupil; nurse & matron. Action begins with one announcing *'I'm leaving.'*

Group Work

It is best to start with simple ideas and small groups, (which are changed for each topic) especially when working with members who may not have done improvisation before. At first, participants may prefer to act as themselves, for in that way they find it easier to concentrate on 'the story' they have been given to work on. In time, they may wish to assume another character even though they may not have been directed to do so. Begin with open titles and remind the players that, as far as possible, they should keep their 'plays' short (no more than five minutes) and try to give the action an introduction (beginning), an event (a middle) and a resolution (an end).

Each section begins with examples of instruction for the players, but as they become more experienced this shouldn't be necessary. Pooling of ideas from within each group is much more valuable. Topics may be taken from a variety of sources. Scenes may be based on

'Open' ideas

Gibberish

(Group of 3). **A** and **B** are working when they have an accident or something goes wrong. **C** arrives and they must convey to him what has happened and what they want him to do, but they may only speak 'gibberish'. It helps if **A** and **B** have used this 'language' from the beginning and established made-up words for certain objects, although **C** will not know these.

Stop, Thief!

(Group of 3). **A** leaves a supermarket. **B** follows him and accuses him of theft. He is taken before **C**, the Manager. What happens? It should not have been decided whether he is guilty or not, so that players gain practice in using argument and persuasion to resolve the situation.

The Visitor

(Group of 4 – 3 family members and 1 visitor who is brought home by a member of the family.) The character of the visitor is very important. What effect does his arrival have on everyone?

The Outsider

(A cohesive group of 4, +1) Consider what makes an outsider. Is he a stranger, a joker, a tramp, over-eager to please or embarrassing (like 'The Office's David Brent)? Is the group jealous of him, is he a prude or is he just 'strange' in some other way? Is he eventually accepted and if so, why/how?

Further 'open' ideas

The following topics may require more planning but give excellent opportunities for collaboration and imagination. Encourage players to invest in original thought and not just to create the obvious (see 'The Journey', below). With some characterisation, the activity generally results in 'a good story'. Be prepared to allow a little more time for these:

The Journey

This can be factual or magical. Decide on the reason and historical period of travel, the mode of transport, the destination and the outcome. You may, for example, decide to journey into another time, or into space where you discover an inhabited planet. In this case, starting as if you're sitting in a time/space capsule about to land is one way of setting the scene. This formation also makes a satisfying way to end this type of play – if you decide (and are able) to return home, of course!

Other starting points

The following could be used as stimuli for activities similar to 'The Journey', above.

• The Picnic	• A Stormy Night	• The Phone Call
• Treasure!	• The Swindle	• My Slave
• Pirate	• Shipwreck	• The Strike
• 'Must Buy' – Plan and film a TV advert for a new product.		

LOCATIONS

THE LIFT

As an imaginary character you enter a lift with others and act out what happens when the lift stops between floors and twenty minutes elapses (not in real time!) before it begins to move again. Do your reactions reveal/match your character? How do you behave when you finally reach the safety of a floor?

THE QUEUE

As some character other than yourself, you stand in a line as if waiting in a very slow supermarket queue. How do you behave and interact with others? What do you say?

THE PLATFORM

Before acting out this scene, assume a character and a mood which you may be in. You're standing on a station platform on the way to an important meeting and the train's very late. How do you feel? What, if anything, do you do and say? How does the scene end?

FURTHER IDEAS

In each of the following, the premise is that one or two players will enter the location and disturb or change the ambience of the others already there:

• A Restaurant	• A Waiting Room	• A Launderette
• A Pub	• A Police Station	• A Haunted Building
• A Beach	• A Railway Carriage	• An Old People's Home
• A Park Bench	• An Infants' Classroom	• A Race Meeting

PLAY-MAKING

This particular kind of simple improvisation, which involves action and reaction, can be repeated many times. To facilitate this, the leader would be wise to create a set of cards – see opposite – which suggest characters and scenarios.

Note: With members new to improvisation, it may be best to use these cards in three stages:

1 Players have only character card, A, and the scenario D.

2. Next time they add a 'mood' card. (ABD).

3. Each player has a character, intention and mood to bring to the given scene (ABCD)

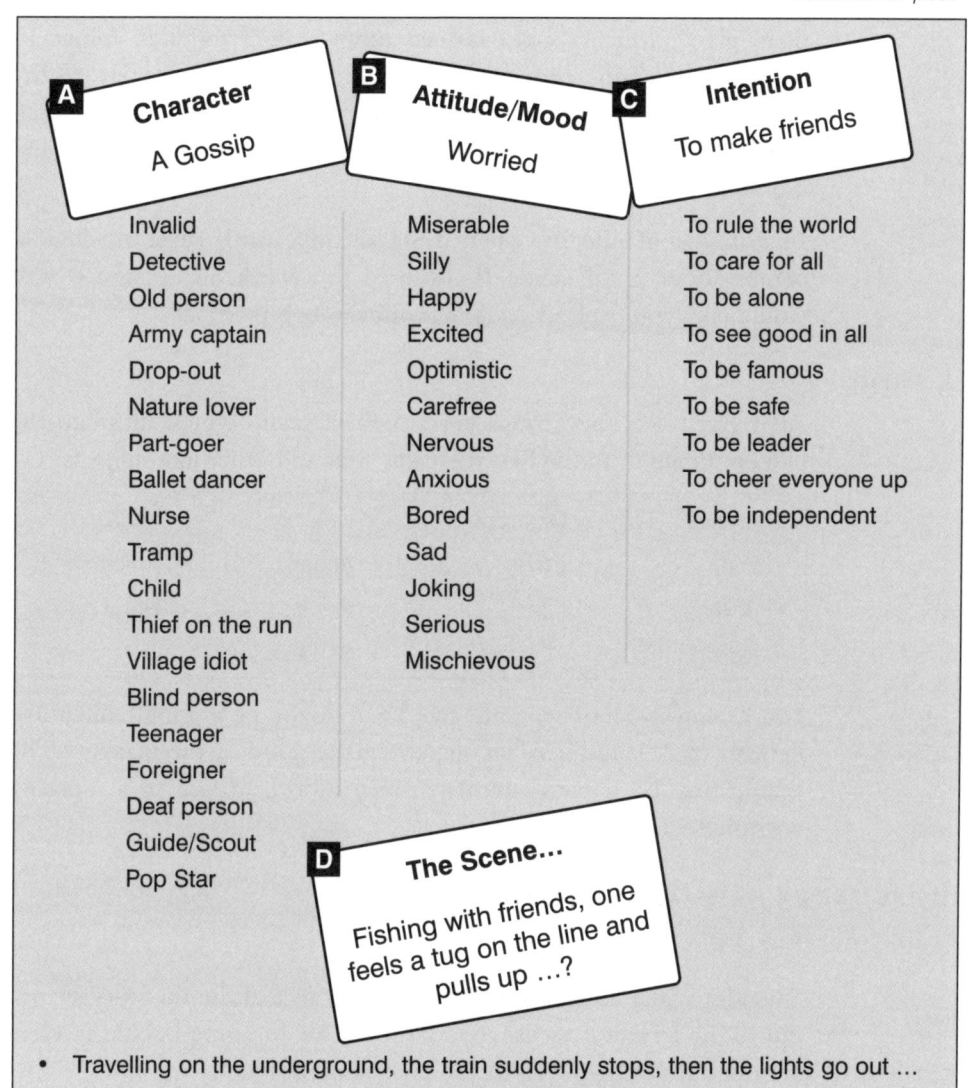

continued on p202

A Character
A Gossip

B Attitude/Mood
Worried

C Intention
To make friends

Character	Attitude/Mood	Intention
Invalid	Miserable	To rule the world
Detective	Silly	To care for all
Old person	Happy	To be alone
Army captain	Excited	To see good in all
Drop-out	Optimistic	To be famous
Nature lover	Carefree	To be safe
Part-goer	Nervous	To be leader
Ballet dancer	Anxious	To cheer everyone up
Nurse	Bored	To be independent
Tramp	Sad	
Child	Joking	
Thief on the run	Serious	
Village idiot	Mischievous	
Blind person		
Teenager		
Foreigner		
Deaf person		
Guide/Scout		
Pop Star		

D The Scene...
Fishing with friends, one feels a tug on the line and pulls up ...?

- Travelling on the underground, the train suddenly stops, then the lights go out ...
- Visiting a busy fair, there's suddenly a shout from a stall nearby ...
- Walking along a quiet country lane, you look over a field gate and see ...?
- Exploring beach caves after a picnic, you discover that you can't find the entrance ...
- Visiting a waxworks, from the corner of your eye, you see one figure move ...
- In the office, someone says 'What's wrong with X?' (a colleague).
- You're looking down on a coffin at an historical dig, when the lid begins to move ...
- You're in your garden with friends when a stranger appears. He looks worried ...
- In a restaurant with friends, you see a man at a nearby table behaving suspiciously ...

When each group of 3, 4 or 5 has been formed, players take an individual card from the relevant pile placed face down. Then each group is given a previously unseen scenario card. This sets the scene which the characters must play out. The groups should choose titles for their 'plays', which should last no more than 5 minutes. Allow 10 minutes preparation time before each group shows their 'play' to the others, their 'audience'. This has proved to be a popular activity, which provides fun and instruction as well as encouraging co-operation and use of the imagination.

As a matter of interest, when using all three cards there are 28,000 combinations in this game. If you used 10 a week, 52 weeks a year, it would take you over 53 years to work through them all!

A Theme

After discussion the groups enact a short scene which illustrate the chosen theme from the Seven Deadly Sins and other like subjects:

• Avarice	• Gluttony	• Lust	• Sloth
• Pride	• Envy	• Anger	• Ambition
• Revenge	• Fear	• Power	• Hope
• Fidelity	• Conflict	• Sacrifice	

For example: Sacrifice. This can be thought of a moral dilemma. Perhaps one character is 'sacrificed' for the good of the majority. The setting may be historic, domestic, recreational, in war or a working environment.

Using known material as a starting point

Fables

The idea when using a story or fable is *not* to recreate the story as it is, but to modernise it or use it to illustrate the meaning behind it. Here are just a few suggestions to use as examples:

The Boy Who Cried Wolf so many times that no-one believed him when he told the truth.

The Ugly Duckling, once an outcast, but who proved to be a beautiful swan.

The Lion and the Mouse who showed that even the most humble could help the powerful.

The Hare and the Tortoise – slow and steady achieves a result.

Quotations

These may come from many sources including verse, fiction or plays. The task in the following is to create a scene suggested by the lines by commenting, asking a question or changing the original thought. Note that you are *not* trying to continue the writer's original idea, but simply using his lines as a springboard for your own interpretation. It does not matter whether you know where the quotes come from, or what comes next. In fact, *not* knowing – and having to take the lines just on face value – may well lead to much more creative improvisations!

- *'Tyger, Tyger, burning bright*
  In the forest of the night ...' (William Blake)
  What shall we do about it?

- *'The Owl and the Pussycat*
  Went to sea in a beautiful pea-green boat...' (Edward Lear)
  But they landed on the wrong island!

- *'Please Sir, can I have some more?' said Oliver.* (Dickens, 'Oliver Twist').
  What shall we do with this child?

- *'Do you remember an inn, Miranda,*
  Do you remember an inn?' ('Tarantella', Hilaire Belloc)
  Now, what happened there?

- *'When shall we three meet again?'* (The Three Witches in Shakespeare's 'Macbeth') The challenge here is to take the spell from the original verse (Act iv sc I) and use it (update it if you wish), but set the scene in another time and place. It could be in the present, it could be anywhere in the world, but the players should know what they hope to achieve by casting the spell. – and do they succeed?

So many of Shakespeare's lines have become part of our language and they make a good starting point for improvisation. We owe the following to him although there are many more, of course. The task is, as before, to create a scene, but this time make the quoted lines the *last* ones in your play:

- *'Neither a borrower nor a lender be,*
  For loan oft loses both itself and friend.' (Polonius to his son in 'Hamlet', Act 1, sc III.)

- *'The course of true love never did run smooth ...'* (Lysander, 'Midsummer Night's Dream' Act 1, sc I.)

- *'O beware, my lord, of jealousy
  It is the green-eyed monster ...'* (Iago warns Othello against his wife, Act 3, sc III.)

- *'Good night, good night, parting is such sweet sorrow ...'* (Juliet, 'Romeo and Juliet' Act 2, sc II.)

TEXTS FOR LARGE GROUPS

These are more ambitious projects for experienced players, but they generally prove to be absorbing topics for the whole group to work on. The work will spread over more than one session, and may even, if later scripted, grow into a public performance! These improvisations call for more thought, planning and discussion as well as characterisation and collaboration.

SNOW WHITE AND THE SEVEN DWARFS

This story could be improvised as it was written, unless the group wants a challenge. In that case, the hero, heroine and the dwarfs could be 'modernised' in some way, as could the work they do, and someone other than a witch could represent the evil in the story – but good should overcome evil in the end.

THE PIED PIPER OF HAMELIN

(by Robert Browning). This could also become a play in its own right. It could begin with groups of townspeople complaining, with another group forming the Council, the Pied Piper as the principal player and others playing the rats and the children.

VISITING

'Welcome,' said their hospitable host ... stepping forward to announce them, 'welcome, gentlemen, to Manor Farm.' (Dickens, 'Pickwick Papers).

This last line in Chapter 5 of Dickens' novel relates to the arrival of Pickwick and his friends at the home of Mr Wardle after a rather adventurous carriage journey, but you are free to interpret the welcome as you wish. Manor Farm may be anywhere and your host can be anyone. Why are you visiting? Act out a scene exploring why you are at the farm and what happens during your visit.

JABBERWOCKY

(from 'Alice through the Looking Glass' by Lewis Carroll). This may be an unexpected suggestion but it can prove to bring out a great deal of imagination as players become 'slithy toves' and 'mome raths'. It is an opportunity to enter the world of fantasy and there is no right or wrong in any interpretation. A Narrator reads the verse as players enact it, so that it becomes a mimed presentation. The use of music greatly adds to the finished scenes.

CRIME AND PUNISHMENT

No, not Dostoevsky! In the following, we take children's stories and set them in a court scene. You will need to appoint a Judge, defence and prosecuting barristers as well as the complainant, the accused, the jury and its foreman. You may even call witnesses. Again, much planning will be needed, but the characterisation should be fun!

Goldilocks and the Three Bears. Father Bear takes Goldilocks to court for breaking and entering.

The Three Little Pigs accuse the Wolf of harassment and take him to court.

Members should be encouraged to think up their own scenarios too – any well-known story or characters can be used as a basis for the creation of mini-plays. The more familiar the original text is, the more fun the group can have with showing the characters in sticky situations that the original author never intended! (However, be aware that if you wish to work any of these ideas up for public performance that some modern characters are very heavily protected as trademarks.)

COSTUME/PROPERTIES WHICH SUGGEST A CHARACTER

The use of one item of clothing or a prop is a useful way of concentrating on characterisation within an improvised scene. In preparation, the leader should supply a variety of objects, or each member could be asked to bring an item – it must be possible to wear the extra clothing over the members' own clothes. Using a book of raffle tickets, each item is numbered with its 'twin' number being folded and placed ready for the draw. Having formed the separate groups, each player draws a ticket and then must use the item he 'wins' to create his character. You may wish to use both an item of clothing and a prop if the groups are small. The scene must be woven round the characters who form the group. Some items you may wish to use are listed over:

> Scarf, shawl, skirts of various lengths, raincoat, jacket, apron, dressing gown, waistcoat – the brighter the better, ankle socks, Wellingtons, slippers, hiking boots, boater, bowler hat, child's cap, baseball cap, clown's hat, ladies hats, bonnets, tiara, pith helmet, cowboy hat.
>
> Handbag, shopping trolley, walking stick, briefcase, basket, magnifying glass, sunglasses, goggles, sweeping brush, bucket, shovel, mop, umbrella, notebook & pencil, sack, dog lead, a cane, fairy wand, – anything which may stir the imagination!

THE BOSS

These are activities to encourage leadership skills and are best used when members are accustomed to working together. There will be among the membership those who always take a leading role or who organise the others. Here, it's suggested that once individual groups have been formed, the leader chooses someone other than the usual 'organiser' from each group who must then be 'in charge'. They will be given instructions, which they must carry out. Knowing the players, the leader can best judge who might be given this opportunity to take an organising position.

- As Captain of a sports team, you must teach your group a routine, which will engender positive thinking before the game.
- You are organising a Fashion Show. Rehearse your new models ready to walk along the cat-walk in (imaginary) garments ready for the display.
- You are leader of a group practising movements which will bring to them calmness and control.
- You have to teach a short dance routine to your group for a musical.
- You are Officer in Charge of some new Army recruits and you must teach them some basic drill.
- Your group is on a secret mission, one which will surprise the enemy. Show them how to advance without being seen and practice this as a team.
- You must teach your group 'The Dance of the Robots'.
- You are in charge of a Keep Fit team about to give a Fitness display. Practice the routine together.
- You are in charge of a Roman galley ship. You must train your oarsmen to move in time by teaching them a rhythmic chant to say as they row.
- As a Circus Trainer, you must teach your group some simple circus skills.

CONCLUSION

All the suggestions for Improvisation above are just that – suggestions. Some will work better than others and many will give rise to other ideas within the group, so that before long you will have a list of ideas of your own which over time, you'll be able to repeat, with variations. Some may even grow into performance material, which is why, if you can, you should keep a record of the work you do. The use of appropriate music, although not suggested here, does help performance. Indeed, some music may even inspire a topic for exciting improvisation, whether it is a modern song or classical music such as that in the compilation for Disney's 'Fantasia'. It is certainly worth using music for a change.

It is to be expected that at first you will make mistakes in your presentation. You'll find it difficult to keep unscripted conversation going without talking over each other; your positioning will lack foresight and you may even work with your back to the audience; you'll mask each other; you may find it hard to work to a satisfactory ending in the given time. But don't despair. These are all part of the learning curve and should prove valuable. Both you and your fellow members who'll be your audience, will recognise these errors, although no criticism will be given – and if it is, it should be no more than a suggestion – 'next time why not try / it might be better if...' Everyone learns best through practical experience, and this along with mutual observation will, over a period of time, teach you some of the stagecraft skills you'll need in performance. As you become more practised, you will remember that the needs of the audience must be taken into account too, particularly in relation to the actual staging and positioning of the actors they're watching.

Above all, however, remember that 'the play's the thing', so the story, with character relationship and interaction, is most important, especially in later group work. Whenever you work together, whether it's to rehearse a show or to 'improvise' you'll have fun and that is the whole point of starting an amateur drama group in the first place.

APPENDIX: USEFUL WEBSITES

Hypertext links to these and other sites can be found on the Eyelevel Books website at www.eyelevelbooks.co.uk/drama

Legal and Statutory Bodies

Information on **lotteries and gaming**
www.bbc.co.uk/actionnetwork   or   www.gbgb.org.uk

Health & Safety Executive, gives practical advice on such matters.
www.hse.gov.uk

Arts Council England is the national development agency for the arts in England and Wales, distributing public money from Government and the National Lottery www.artscouncil.org.uk
The Scottish Arts Council can be found at www.scottisharts.org.uk
The Arts Council of Northern Ireland is at www.artscouncil-ni.org

The Charity Commission is the regulator for charities in England and Wales, for information on charitable status www.charity-commission.gov.uk
The Office of the Scottish Charity Regulator can be found at www.oscr.org.uk
At the time of writing, there is no equivalent body in Northern Ireland

The **MCPS-PRS Alliance** is the home of the world's best songwriters, composers and music publishers and has information on licences for public performances of copyright music. See also www.ppluk.com (the Phonographic Performance Limited site) www.mcps-prs-alliance.co.uk/

Sources of General Help and Inspiration

The British and International Federation of Festivals for Music, Speech and Dance. www.festivals.demon.co.uk

Online Sound Effects has a library of useful FX at www.sounddogs.com

UK theatre web is worth checking out if you own your own venue
www.uktw.co.uk

The Independent Theatre Council (ITC) is the UK's leading management association for the performing arts, representing around 700 organisations across the UK. www.itc-arts.org.

Amdram is a free website for the amateur theatre community. It includes free resources for groups and individuals interested in amateur theatre. www.amdram.co.uk

National Operatic and Dramatic Association gives a shared voice to the amateur theatre sector, helps amateur societies and individuals achieve the highest standards of best practice and performance and provides leadership and advice to enable the amateur theatre sector to tackle the challenges and opportunities of the 21st century. www.noda.org.uk

NAYT (National Association of Youth Theatres) supports the development of youth theatre activity through training, advocacy, participation programmes and information services. www.nayt.org.uk

SOURCES OF PLAYS AND OTHER MATERIAL

Nick Hern Books is the UK's leading specialist publisher of plays, screenplays and theatrebooks
www.nickhernbooks.co.uk

Samuel French Ltd is THE theatre bookshop and supplier of scripts
www.samuelfrench-london.co.uk

Josef Weinberger is another major supplier of play scripts, musicals and opera
www.josef-weinberger.com

The Internet Theatre Bookshop has a catalogue of plays and texts and a whole lot more! www.stageplays.co.uk

INDEX

Accidents	88
Acquiring skills	141
Actor's notes	125
Advertising	42,45
Apron	61
Articulation	167
Arts Council	17
Assistant stage manager	89,92
Audibility	111
Audition	45,100
notice	100
Backcloth	70
Backstage crew	91,118
Banners	40
Blocking	63,104,112,125
Body language	115,175
Box office	35
Box set	69
Breath control	164
Budget	53,60,124
Candles, use on stage	82
Casting the play	100
Character	112
finding	106,115,127–131
Choreographer	85
Christmas show	55
Church (hall)	31
Cloakroom	49
Colour	71,118
Committee	14
Competitions	43
Concentration	154
Confidence	174
Constitution	7,13,15
Copyright	27,60
Costs, hiring venue	58
of production	33
Costume	59,67,118
Crew, backstage	118

Criminal Records Bureau	8
Cuts to text	27
Cyclorama (cyc)	63
Deputy stage manager	89,92,120
Dialect	57,85
Director	65,66
as actor	94
role of	94
Drama festivals	32
Dress rehearsal	89
Drinking, on stage	84
Emotion, showing	137,166
End stage	30
Energy	180
Entrances and exits	58,97,179
Eye contact	116,176
Farce	57
Fight designer	86
Finance	65
Fire doors	47
exits	88
hazard	70
use on stage	82
Firearms, use on stage	83
First night	47,122,137
Flats	62
Fliers	40,45
Flowers and plants, on stage	82
Food, on stage	84
Front of House	46,47
Fund-raising	17
Funding	16
Furnishings	99
Furniture	66,69,106
FX	63
Gels	75
Gesture	116,178

Get in	64,89,118	Members	14-15
Get out	64	in considering a play	56
Gobo	75	Membership	5
Group meeting	19	adults	6
first	13,20	children	8
format	21	fees	7
venue	9	rules	16
when	11	Memory	133,181
Group name	12	Mime	183,185
Grouping, of actors on stage	106,115	Moves	105,115
		Music, incidental	77
House lights	120	pre-show	76,120
		Musicals	53,54
Ice-breakers	144	Musician	85
Imagination	147,181		
Improvisation	183,192	Name (of group)	12
Inflection	171	Notes	117
Insurance	11		
Intention	174	Objectives	4
Internet	44	Open air theatre	32
Intonation	117		
		Pace	105,171
Last night	122	Pageant	54
Licence, alcohol	49	Pauses	172
availability	59	Permissions, (copyright)	26,53
fees	28	Pitch of voice	170
Lighting	63	Play casting	100
designer	67	considering	25,29,55
effects	99	genre	56
equipment	58,76	study of	95
technician	74	reading	4,25
types	75	Poster	45
Lines, forgetting	136	design	37
learning	113,132	distribution	40
Lottery	18	Posture	162,177
LX	63,76	Power (vocal)	171
		Press, articles	42
Make-up	121	release	41
Marketing	37	Producer	65
audience-based	46	Production, choice of	53
further aspects	42	team	66
timetable	45	timetable	45
Masking	63,115	manager	67

meeting	99	equipment	58,78-79
profiles	65	technician	76
Programme, layout	41	Space activities	146
Projection	173	Spacing, of actors on stage	115
Prompt	92	Sponsorship	18,45
corner	61	Spotlights	74
Props	79-84,137	Stage, types of	29,63
storage of	58	Stage directions	104
Publicity	37,124	Stage manager	48,68,87-91,120
		deputy	61
Radio, local	44	Staging a production	29
Raffle	18,49,55	Steering group	4,9
Read through	111	Street theatre	32
Refreshments	49	Strike	64,91
Rehearsal, dress	89,117,122	Strobe	75
first	112	Studio space	29
schedule	107		
technical	89,119	Talks	23
timing	109	Team spirit	110
Rehearsals	69,93,125	choosing	142
Relaxation	159	Technical rehearsal	89
head and neck	162	Telephones, use on stage	82
Reviews	44,45	Theatre in the round	31
Revue	54	visits	23
Royalties	28	Thrust stage	30
		Tickets	34
Scenery	62	concessionary	34
Script	25,102,125	free	36
for director	95	pricing	34,38
marking up	95,132	printing	45
Seating	48	sales	35
capacity	58	Tone (of voice)	171
Second night	122	Treasurer	14
Set	59,68,111	Tunnel	62
designer	67,69,97	Type casting	104
Set up (get in)	64		
Sitting	180	Upstaging	63
Sketches	24		
Smoking	83	Venue, production	58
Sound	63	Video recording	28
check	78	Vocal projection	136
designer	67	skills	164
effects	77,99		

Walking	177
Wardrobe	71
Warm-ups	21, 144
Wheelchair access	36, 48
Wigs	73
Windows, stage	97
Wing space	58
Wings	61
Writing	24